INTRODUCTION TO WITTGENSTEIN'S TRACTATUS LOGICO-PHILOSOPHICUS

FRIEDRICH HÜLSTER

TRANSLATED FROM THE GERMAN BY W. E. O'HEA

EDITED BY INGRID TRUEMPER AND KLAUS TRUEMPER

Copyright © 2019 by Klaus Truemper
All rights reserved.

Softcover published by
Leibniz Company
2304 Cliffside Dr
Plano, Texas, 75023
USA

Original Edition March 2017
Updated Edition 2018
Second Updated Edition 2019

No part of this book may be reproduced, or stored in a retrieval system, or transmitted in any form or by any means, electronic, mechanical, photocopying, recording, or otherwise, without express permission of the publisher.

Cover Art:
The editors gratefully acknowledge permission by NASA, ESA, and STScI to use the photo *Galactic Center* taken by the Hubble Telescope.

Library of Congress Cataloging-in-Publication Data

Hülster, Friedrich, 1905–1992
    Introduction to Ludwig Wittgenstein's *Tractatus Logico-Philosophicus* / Friedrich Hülster
    translator O'Hea, W. E.
    editors Truemper, Ingrid and Truemper, Klaus
  Includes bibliographical references and subject index.
  ISBN 978-0-9663554-4-4
  1. Wittgenstein Tractatus Logico-Philosophicus.
  2. Introduction

Table of Contents

Editors' Note 1

Author's Preface 6

Overview 8

Chapter 1 The World 10

    1.1 The World Common to All Men   10
    1.2 Things and Facts   12
    1.3 Elementary Things and Elementary Facts   16
    1.4 Properties   19
    1.5 Logical Form of Things   23
    1.6 Essential Unconnectedness of Facts   25
    1.7 Things, the Substance of the World   28

Chapter 2 Communication 31

    2.1 Means of Communication   31
    2.2 Wittgenstein's Picture Theory   33
    2.3 Wittgenstein's Idea of a Picture   34
    2.4 True and False Pictures   38
    2.5 Logical Form Common to Picture and Reality   39
    2.6 Form of Representation   40
    2.7 Thoughts and Speech Propositions   41
    2.8 Elements and Structure of Verbal Pictures   43
    2.9 Elementary Propositions   45
    2.10 Precise Definition of the Tractatus Problem   47
    2.11 Intellectual Value of the Picture Theory   50

Chapter 3 Efficiency of Speech 53

    3.1 Peculiarities of Picture Components   54
    3.2 Simple Propositions   56
    3.3 Negation in Simple Propositions   63
    3.4 Compound Propositions by Logical Operations   64
    3.5 Universal Propositions   71
    3.6 Propositions About Intentions   73

Chapter 4 Misuse of Language 77

    4.1 Colloquial and Scientific Misuses   77
    4.2 Traditional Philosophy   78
    4.3 Inadmissibility of Philosophical Propositions   80
    4.4 Inadmissible Questions   85

Chapter 5 Genuine Philosophy 89

    5.1 Tasks of Philosophy   89
    5.2 Philosophy and the Tractatus   90

Appendix A Time Relations in Physics 94

Appendix B Elementary Things and Facts 96

References 97

About Author and Translator 99

    About the Author   99
    About the Translator   101

Subject Index 102

Editors' Note

The editors of this book are a grandniece and nephew of author Friedrich Hülster. After the death of Hülster in 1992 and his wife Eva Hülster in 1996, the nephew received from the executor of the estate a large box containing Hülster's writing about philosophy, all of which is in German.

The box included an introduction to Wittgenstein's *Tractatus Logico-Philosophicus*, which we had known about, but also, rather unexpectedly, an English translation by W. E. O'Hea. This book is based on that material.

The delay in issuing this book has a simple explanation. For many years, it was not clear how the material could be published, since it seemed unlikely that a publisher would anticipate sufficient profit to print the material.

But that is no longer a concern. Books can now be efficiently printed and distributed via the Internet.

The editors have freely modified the text to clarify or revise statements, and to update the spelling to US English.

Citations of Wittgenstein's *Tractatus Logico-Philosophicus* are based on a 1961 edition that contains the translation by D. F. Pears and B. F. McGuinness. Wittgenstein assigned decimal numbers to paragraphs. Citations use these numbers even when just a portion of the material is quoted. Here and there, we have adjusted a citation to achieve a US English version that, we hope, properly represents the original German version of the *Tractatus Logico-Philosophicus*.

To keep the presentation uncluttered, the modifications of the translation by O'Hea as well as of the *Tractatus Logico-Philosophicus* citations are not specially marked.

As an aside, the *Tractatus Logico-Philosophicus* is available free of charge from several websites; just google "Wittgenstein Tractatus free pdf."

About Wittgenstein's Tractatus

In 1921, Ludwig Josef Johann Wittgenstein (1889-1951) published a landmark book in philosophy, the *Tractatus Logico-Philosophicus*. The book, now often just called the *Tractatus*, puts forth a picture theory of the meaning of language. There is little doubt that Wittgenstein would have been upset by this characterization. He would have been right, too. There is no brief way to characterize the main hypotheses and conclusions of the Tractatus. But clearly a key goal, if not *the* key goal of Wittgenstein, was to help the reader avoid errors of philosophy.

By 1929, Wittgenstein realized that important arguments of the Tractatus were not correct. Indeed, in the subsequent book *Philosophical Investigations* published in 1953 shortly after his death—followed by a number of additional books assembled later from his notes by his students—he set out to describe methods that, just as intended by the Tractatus, help the reader avoid errors of philosophy. But the approach had drastically changed.

In the preface of the *Philosophical Investigations*, he wrote that the Tractatus contained "grave mistakes." Despite Wittgenstein's harsh assessment, the Tractatus has been reprinted time and again. There is good reason: Understanding the explanations put forth in the Tractatus and then reading the *Philosophical Investigations* and realizing why certain arguments are incorrect, is an excellent way to see why determination of the meaning of language is so complicated.

Amazingly, some current methods of Artificial Intelligence for the computation of meaning of language implicitly assume certain parts of the Tractatus to be correct that according to results in the *Philosophical Investigations* are in error. Accordingly, any such method must fail.

Why You May Want to Read This Book

If you are a person whose profession is not philosophy, and if you are interested in the fundamental question "What can be expressed by language?" then this book is a good way to start an investigation of that question.

It is written by a physicist who for many years was baffled by the fact that language is frequently abused. He then decided to focus on the above question. He started out by studying the works of Wittgenstein, who had dedicated most of his life trying to answer this question.

Don't be deterred from reading this book by the fact that Wittgenstein later refuted the Tractatus. Actually, he desired to publish the Tractatus together with the *Philosophical Investigations*, so that the reader could see how the two works are related.

Wittgenstein is considered by some the most important philosopher of the 20th century. Indeed, the Tractatus is a work of genius. Reading this little book about the Tractatus, you will not just understand the main arguments in that profound work of Wittgenstein, but—as an important side effect—you will also learn how to recognize and cope with the nonsensical statements that swirl around us and try to confuse us.

If reading this book motivates you to delve further into Wittgenstein's works, then that is another positive effect.

Other Introductions and Commentaries

Numerous introductory books and commentaries exist about Wittgenstein's Tractatus. When you google "Introduction Wittgenstein Tractatus," many references appear, some of them recently published.

Examples are G. E. M. Anscombe, *An Introduction to Wittgenstein's Tractatus*; Eli Friedlander, *Signs of Sense*; Howard O. Mounce, *Wittgenstein's Tractatus*; Alfred Nordmann, *Wittgenstein's Tractatus*; Roger M. White, *Wittgenstein's 'Tractatus Logico-Philosophicus'*. These texts are important contributions in philosophy and quite complex, even when described as introductory.

In contrast, this book is not a technical work in philosophy, in fact is not intended for the specialist. There is no attempt of completeness of approach. But the book does bring out the fundamental ideas of Wittgenstein's Tractatus.

In the Author's Preface, which immediately follows this note, Hülster cites the book *Wittgenstein und die moderne Philosophie* (Wittgenstein and Modern Philosophy) by Justus Hartnack as an outstanding example of a short, clear, and concise commentary of the Tractatus that is accessible to nonspecialists. The book is indeed excellent, but also really brief. It explains the Tractatus in just 45 pages of small format.

An even shorter and but also excellent introduction to the Tractatus is provided in the book *Wittgenstein's Conception of Philosophy* of K. T. Fann.

In contrast, Hülster covers the Tractatus at a more leisurely pace, includes many examples, and writes from the viewpoint of a physicist instead of a philosopher.

Acknowledgements

Thanks are due to a number of people who assisted in the publication. M. Opperud and U. Truemper reviewed a first version of the book and suggested changes. B. Scheidegger and J. Trümper provided data about the author and the translator. M. Hittinger helped with technical aspects of the typesetting. The University of Texas at Dallas generously supported this effort; special thanks are due to Provost B. Wildenthal.

Last but not Least

Since we made numerous changes in the translated text, any errors in this book, of whatever kind, are ours alone.

I. T. and K. T.
Summer 2015

Author's Preface

These notes had their origin in a habit of mine—dating from long before I became acquainted with Wittgenstein's book—of never being sure of understanding anything until I could write it down in my own words. It seemed worthwhile to apply this method to the Tractatus. When I began writing, I was not yet aware of the existence of commentaries on the Tractatus which are not only profound but easily understood. An outstanding example is the short book *Wittgenstein und die moderne Philosophie* (Wittgenstein and Modern Philosophy) by Justus Hartnack.

Is it still worthwhile today, so many years after its first appearance in 1921, to work through the Tractatus, if one isn't a professional philosopher? Didn't Wittgenstein himself at a later date, particularly in his *Philosophical Investigations*—written between 1936 and 1949 and published posthumously in 1953—move away from his earlier work and even subject it to sharp criticism?

Indeed, the later work of Wittgenstein is more general in content than the Tractatus, since it treats the informational statements covered by the Tractatus as one among many possible language games. Furthermore, the method of research and exposition used in the *Philosophical Investigations* has little in common with that of the Tractatus.

Both books agree to a great extent in their practically important conclusions. In fact, the warning against the misuse of language becomes more insistent in the *Philosophical Investigations*, and the rejection of philosophy as a doctrine more radical.

Wittgenstein's later work, although written almost entirely in everyday words and phrases, is not easy to understand. The reader will hardly succeed in fathoming that material without having first worked through the Tractatus.

Friedrich Hülster
Louveciennes, France, July 1969

Overview

The first three chapters describe the main results of the Tractatus regarding the role and limits of human language.

Chapter 1 begins with the definition of "world." According to that definition, the world of the Tractatus consists of everything that we can communicate about. That world consists of things and facts that by analysis can be reduced to elementary things and elementary facts.

Chapter 2 examines the representation of the world by pictures, for example, geographical maps and technical drawings. Specifically, things and facts of the world are tied to picture elements and their relations. If such a picture is to be a correct one, the relationships among things and facts of the world on one hand, and among the elements and relations of the picture on the other hand, must—in a certain sense—be in agreement: Wittgenstein says that they must have the same *logical form.*

Chapter 3 uses these results to analyze the human thought processes that find their expression in propositions of language. The chapter shows that every such thought—and thus the corresponding proposition of language—is a combination of pictures, each of which depicts parts of the world, that is, things and facts.

The main conclusion of the first three chapters can be expressed as follows: *A meaningful proposition—no matter how complex—can only depict things and facts of the world.*

Chapter 4 applies this result to philosophy and shows that many philosophical claims are meaningless. This is demonstrated using pseudoproblems of philosophy—that is, problems where the formulation is already meaningless.

So what role is then left for philosophy to play?

Chapter 5 gives Wittgenstein's answer: Philosophy is to help achieve clarity when language is misused in meaningless questions and claims.

Chapter 1

The World

1.1 The World Common to All Men

The *Tractatus Logico-Philosophicus*, hence simply referred to as *Tractatus*, begins with statements about the world. One could also say that the book indirectly outlines what it means by "world." We will ignore that aspect for the moment and instead explore the use of "world" in an informal discussion.

On the one hand, the concept of "world" is so broad that it escapes direct definition, like the concepts of consciousness and existence. On the other hand, "world" is not simply the same as "everything." Hence, we can only elucidate the concept of "world" by pointing to particular aspects, and thus obtain limits of its use.

The word can be used in quite different senses. Among these, we must disregard its often quite arbitrary use in everyday language where, for example, it is applied to the earth or turns up in metaphors like the "world of sounds." Yet even if we confine ourselves to science and philosophy, we find the concept of "world" occurring with sharply differing emphasis upon its individual aspects, as in the following examples.

The World We Live In. This is the title of a book by Lincoln Barnett. The chapters cover nature: its origins, its laws, and its structure from heavenly bodies down to microbes.

"The world of primitive man" and "The world views of 18th-century philosophers." Here a quite different aspect of the world concerns various human groups.

"An aging man ceases to understand the world." In this phrase from Jean Amery's book *On Aging*, the world is primarily a process in which the individual is involved.

"The world created by God." Here "world" particularly stresses the idea of something which could exist in some other form or not exist at all.

In contrast, the world of the Tractatus is the same for all thinking beings, the one about which their thoughts, if rightly formed, must coincide. This presupposes that thoughts are communicable. Consequently, the world only includes what can be the object of communicable thoughts.

At this point, we find ourselves already in the midst of the problems dealt with in the Tractatus. Indeed, it is by no means obvious what is communicable. How far does this include man's subjective activities, his imagination, his sensations and his feelings? Also, not every object about which we can think and communicate necessarily belongs to the world; we must also find such an object actually present in the world. And just what do we mean by "finding it present"?

No problem arises with physical things such as plants, animals, or houses. However, we can think and speak about centaurs, yet they do not belong to the world. Must we then count our idea of centaurs as part of the world?

Quite clearly, we do not find hexagonal circles or wooden iron in the world, though we can say something even about these objects; that is, that the idea of them is self-contradictory.

There are still more difficult questions. What about numbers and geometrical figures, or any kind of ideal objects? What about natural laws? What about the human soul?

The above concept of "world" therefore leads us to ontological questions—that is, questions about the most general characteristics of everything that exists.

Questions of this kind are not, however, Wittgenstein's aim. In the Tractatus, he deals with something that looks much more modest—that is, the nature of communication. How is information passed on? What conditions must our speech comply with so that genuine information is transferred? Lastly, what can be so conveyed?

Of course, the knowledge we want to convey influences the process in which we convey it, and conversely. We thus are faced with the question, where and how we will begin our inquiry into the nature of communication.

It seems simplest that we begin with some—possibly vague—idea of what we want to convey. For this reason, Wittgenstein puts the world at the beginning of his considerations. It follows that complete answers to the above metaphysical questions are not to be expected when the idea of "world" is first introduced. But as we accompany Wittgenstein in the course of the inquiry, we will gain some insight regarding those questions.

1.2 Things and Facts

We first take a look with Wittgenstein at the world and observe to what extent its parts are common, or at least capable of becoming common, to all thinking persons.

The condition of commonality is that human beings are able to form an identical judgement. In other words, they can discuss common parts with one another without being at cross purposes.

Now we find in the world *things* and *facts*. We cover these concepts next, beginning with *things*.

We can divide things into two groups.

First, there are easily understood things, that is, things that we either perceive directly, like houses, human beings, and planets. Or things whose existence we conclude from their effects upon things that we do perceive; examples are atoms, electromagnetic waves, and animals that existed in earlier ages of the earth.

1.2 Things and Facts

Human beings can reach agreement about all such things through the exchange of information.

Second, there are things which obviously exist, but about which we are unable to convey satisfactorily intelligible information to anyone. Our own sense perceptions, pains, and feelings belong to this class.

The color in our field of vision when we look at a cloudless sky, and what makes it different from the color impression when we look at an orange, are things that we cannot explain to anyone else, not even by pointing to a color chart. For we do not know what the other person experiences when looking at the same things.

If we describe to someone a pain in our shoulder as being acute, dull, or shooting, then that person can only vaguely guess what experience of her own may perhaps correspond to it.

Next we cover the concept of *facts*.

In the world, we find *relations between existing things*. Between the earth and the sun, there exists the relation that the earth is smaller than the sun, and also the relation that the earth goes around the sun. Between Plato and Socrates, there is the relation that Plato was younger than Socrates, and also that he was a pupil of Socrates.

Wittgenstein calls relations between things *facts*.

It is easier for us to understand one another when we talk about relations or connections between things—that is, about facts, than when we talk about the things themselves.

In most cases, a thing has many characteristics. We can only mention a few and do not know whether these are the essential ones for the person we are talking with. For a mechanic, a car consists of wheels, axles, pistons, and so on. For a scrap dealer, a car consists of steel, brass, and aluminum, together with a few worthless pieces of textiles and plastics.

In contrast, we can express ourselves with unmistakable clarity about facts within our knowledge, even if we have no effective knowledge of the things connected by the facts. For instance, when we say, "The pills are in the blue box; they relieve headaches," we are always correctly understood. Yet we may not have the slightest idea what these pills are made of.

In the past, people agreed about the facts that make up thermodynamics—for example, that heat passes between bodies of different temperatures—long before agreement could be reached about the thing called heat.

The distinction between information concerning things and information concerning facts comes out clearly in the different way we speak of the two sorts of information. We say that we communicate a fact, but we cannot say that we communicate a thing. We only communicate something *about* a thing when we describe it.

The two ideas of *things* and *facts* can no more be defined than the idea of the *world* discussed earlier. Philosophers call such ideas *categories*.

To define any idea, we must state the more general class into which it falls (*genus proximum*) and what special characteristics (*differentia specifica*) distinguish it from the rest of the class. For example, a rhombus is a parallelogram whose sides are equal.

Now a category cannot be defined in this way, nor in either of the following two ways of definition, which at any rate are not always considered to be admissible. These two ways are, first, an enumeration of the characteristics of an idea and, second, an enumeration of all the objects to which it applies.

In Wittgenstein's view, everything that exists in the world can be included in one or other of the two categories called things and facts. This may astonish us. For example, properties of things, such as being hard or green, appear to be neither things nor facts. Where does human behavior such as honesty or constancy belong? What about numbers and other subject matter of mathematics? What about logic relations such as negation? What about properties and property-like attributes ascribed to persons? What about abstract ideas? In short, what about everything that since the time of Plato has been included in the category of *ideal objects*?

As for *ideal objects*, it will become clear in the course of our inquiry where they belong. But a look ahead is useful: Ideal objects in the sense of things that we find in the world, do not exist; they do not form part of what we can state about the world, but are part of the process of making statements.

So how do we accomplish the description of a thing? The things we encounter in the world are mostly not simple, but composed of other things that are their constituent parts. Even these latter parts are in most cases made up of other things. For example, a tree is composed of a trunk, large and small branches, and leaves; the leaves are made up of nerves and leaf tissue; the leaf tissue is made of cells, which in turn consist of nucleus, plasm, and membrane; and so on.

When we describe a complex thing, in our mind we take it apart into pieces. By so doing, we discover new things which are its constituent parts; we then stop considering the complex thing and focus on the constituents. We also discover relations connecting these new things. These relations are facts. For example, branches *end in* leaves, plasm *surrounds* the nucleus of the cell.

The further we continue the process of description, the more we split up constituent parts into their sub-constituent parts. At the same time, we state the facts linking the larger units to the smaller ones. At the end, we have obtained a chain of facts. The original thing and its components have gradually faded out of our statements, leaving finally the last sub-sub-constituents when we are unable to carry out further analysis.

In the example of the tree, the final components would be the constituent parts of the cells or atoms.

When the analysis stops, we only have names for the final components, and no further information about them.

1.3 Elementary Things and Elementary Facts

The description of any complex thing comes to a stop when we reach a stage of analysis beyond which our knowledge ceases. Wittgenstein, however, is of the opinion that there is a limit to the possible analysis of things that is independent of our knowledge. In this postulate, Wittgenstein follows the trend of thought called *atomism* that was introduced by the philosopher Democritus (circa 460–370 BCE). Atomism received triumphant verification in the natural sciences during the 20th century.

According to Wittgenstein's postulate, in every analytical description we are bound to reach at last *elementary things* that cannot be further analyzed and that we can only name. Our statements about these things are confined to mentioning the relations in which they occur—that is, the *elementary facts*. Appendix B tells why we use the term "elementary" here.

Naturally, one would like to see a practical example where the analytical description of a thing is continued down to elementary things and elementary facts. However, Wittgenstein gives no such example and—according to notes in his diary—concluded that he could not do so.

Yet he believes that, even if he succeeded in proving that analysis of this kind practically cannot be carried out, the theoretical possibility of such analysis still would follow from logical arguments.

He is certain that there is a limit to the analyzability of things; just as for a mathematician, the total value of a converging infinite series exists even if it cannot be found with step by step calculations.

To understand the difficulty of reaching elementary things, we must bear in mind that Wittgenstein's atomism, also called *logical atomism*, is much wider in scope than physical theory. First, it covers not only all physical things, but also all mental things capable of being the object of communication. Second, it requires an analysis pushed much farther than the physicist normally undertakes.

Given these considerations, we must expect that the analytical description of the world contains things other than physical elementary things—for instance, simplest space-time occurrences such as *rotation* or *momentary movement in a straight line*, as well as simple space or time relations like *bigger than*, *beside*, or *earlier than*.

We emphasize that in Wittgenstein's phraseology the *existence* of a relation between two things is a fact, but that a relation *by itself* is not a fact but a thing. To call such dissimilar matters *things* may seem rather artificial. In *Hauptströmungen der Gegenwartsphilosophie* (Mainstream Contemporary Philosophy), Wolfgang Stegmüller uses for the latter things the expression *not-facts*. But that definition is open to the objection that ideal objects then are not-facts as well. Yet Wittgenstein does not include them among things.

An example illustrates the concepts. "Plato" and "Socrates" denote things. The relation "was younger than" is a thing as well. Then "Plato was younger than Socrates" is a fact. Note that this fact can be viewed as a sequence of three things: Plato, "was younger than", Socrates.

Our physical knowledge of atoms furnishes us with a good working model of Wittgenstein's logical atomistic theory, in spite of the differences between them. In physics, we have pushed the analytical description down to elements that cannot be further analyzed, but whose relations can be indicated.

At the same time, we cannot do more than just give names to the elements themselves.

Physics also shows us how things that once passed for being elementary may dissolve under further analysis into things yet more elementary and related to one another by new facts.

When the Tractatus appeared, atomic nuclei and electrons were regarded as the ultimate building blocks of matter that could be named, but whose nature could not be stated. What could be stated were facts in which they occurred, such as their *mutual* attraction or the distances *between them* inside the atom.

Since then, the complex theory of atomic nuclei, with their neutrons, mesons, etc. and the intricate facts about how these are packed together and how much energy they hold, has become tragically famous through the development of nuclear weapons. Despite such detailed insight, we still cannot predict where further analysis will lead us. But some physicists hope that someday we shall come up against particles which are absolutely and finally elementary.

It is difficult to understand why Wittgenstein thought it so important that in the logical analysis of all the things in the world we should come upon an absolute limit.

If the limit were dependent upon the knowledge we have at the moment—in much the same way as is the case today in the natural sciences—this would not make much difference to his philosophy. Indeed, it would not influence the account of his views given here. For every stage of knowledge, it would remain true that the world—common to all because we can inform one another about it—contains only facts.

The ultimate frame of reference of facts—that is, the elementary things—remains in the dark. This is the meaning of the first two sentences of the Tractatus:

> *The world is all that is the case.* (Tractatus 1)

> *The world is the totality of facts, not of things.* (Tractatus 1.1)

The precedence of facts over things is completely familiar to the physicist when research goals are defined. For instance, to the physicist it would be beside the point to ask what kind of things electricity and magnetism are; the task is completed when one can state in an exhaustive manner the connection of electrical phenomena with one another and the relations between electrical and magnetic phenomena.

1.4 Properties

Suppose in the analytical description of some things we finally come upon things that cannot be further analyzed. Can we really say nothing else about these things other than that they are frames of reference for certain relations and connections? Can't we at least state their properties? After all, properties such as being hard, round, or blue play an essential part in the description of things we commonly encounter. On the other hand, Democritus already held that the atoms of the physical world must be propertyless.

In reality, if we found properties in them, we would be tempted to explain them. To do this, we would have to suppose that the so-called elementary particles are composed of still more elementary ones. As long as we imagined the atoms of physics to be like little balls, we were unable to avoid the curious question: What might be inside them?

Likewise, the essence of Wittgenstein's elementary things is that they are without properties. Indeed, the properties of complex things can be decomposed by analytical description and replaced by facts in one of two ways. First, the facts are relations between the things under consideration and other things. Second, the facts are relations between component parts of the things considered.

Often, the derivation of the facts is easily done.

For instance, the first of the two alternatives occurs with the property of being poisonous. When we call a plant *poisonous*, we mean that its use is harmful to people or animals. This interpretation suffices to define the property, since an island never reached by plant-eating creatures would have no poisonous plants.

An example of the second alternative is the property of being *rusty*. A piece of rusty iron consists of a pure metallic iron core and a surface layer of oxides. Neither of these two components can itself be called rusty.

But there are also properties that at first sight can hardly be reduced to anything else, whether things or facts. These are the properties that we experience directly and do not identify by an act of judgement—properties such as *blue, hot, loud,* or *heavy*. Such designations are used with two different meanings, as follows.

First, to denote our sense impressions of things. For instance, *blue* is then what the sky or the forget-me-not flower looks like, and *hot* is when our hand touches a steaming cup of coffee.

Second, to denote things of the physical world. *Blue* is then light with a wavelength between 450 and 495 nanometers that undergoes a characteristic refraction in a prism. A body is *hot* if a thermometer touching it goes up. Generally, properties of the second case can be determined independently of our sense impressions by means of instruments for observation or measurement. If need be, this can be done without human intervention—for example, when a space probe measures the temperature on Venus.

The same names are used for properties in both of these meanings, since in earlier stages of civilization our actual sense impressions of properties were attributed to things existing independently of us. In everyday life, that still happens even now.

1.4 Properties

For example, we may say, "The sun is hot today," meaning that today we feel particularly hot due to the sun.

Nevertheless, we know that our sense impressions are reactions to events in the world outside us, and also that a particular sensation does not always arise from the same external event. For example, if we have been gazing at length at a red surface, then immediately afterward a sheet of paper that normally would look white appears to be greenish. In general, sugar tastes sweet, but with certain diseases it tastes bitter.

Due to these considerations, we cannot know in principle what the sense impressions in the minds of other persons are like—for instance, what the blue sky looks like to them. For this reason, in a driver's test one must make sure that the candidate can distinguish between red and green traffic lights.

We conclude that directly perceived properties of things are something in the mind of the person who experiences them, as are memories and feelings. We could say that these properties signify something in the pictures that appear in our mind as we experience things.

Suppose we analyze a complex thing and wonder how its properties could be reduced to something other than properties—that is, to things or facts. Then we first must state clearly whether we are talking about constituent parts of physical things, or about the images of them that appear in our minds.

It is obvious that the properties of physical things are reducible to facts in any analytical description of such things, since instruments for observing and measuring can only record facts. For example, a spectroscope pointed at a blue sky registers the shorter wavelength of the received light rays, but does not tell anything about the blue that we see.

In physics, all qualitative data have gradually been resolved into quantitative ones. Indeed, in today's physics, it isn't even possible without fear of contradiction to associate the fundamental building blocks of matter with a shape in space; they can only be characterized by their behavior.

More problematic is the analytical description of the things in our consciousness, which are pictures of appearances. These things also turn out to be complex and reducible to components, as follows.

Many properties of a given mental picture can be described in terms of facts. For instance, in our visual picture of a rusty piece of iron, we can mention that a number of irregular spots occur next to each other on the surface. Moreover, more than one organ of our senses often contributes to the picture of an experience.

For example, a picture that may seem entirely optical includes in most cases sensations of muscle movement or position. An instance is our sense impression that a thing is *spherical*. It includes the fact that for all movements of the head, the shape of the boundary of the thing is seen to remain the same. In contrast, the sense impression that a thing is *disc-shaped* includes the fact that by moving either the head or the hand holding the object, we can reduce its shape from a circle to a line.

In the analysis of complex pictures of phenomena, we generally reach irreducible component parts much sooner than in the analysis of physical objects. At the same time, these irreducible component parts may still have properties. How can we eliminate the properties by yet another reduction?

Let's analyze an example. Suppose we look at the green surface of a leaf and think of it as split up into tiny elementary surfaces, lying side by side in our field of vision. Then in spite of this subdivision, every one of these elements is still green.

But is the greenness of the elementary surfaces, which are at the limit where we still distinguish them, really still a property? Are we using the word "property" in the same sense as elsewhere if we apply it to a point in our visual field? We could equivalently say: "There is greenness at this point of our visual field." In other words, the colors we see are already part of the basic elements of the field of vision, and can rightly be called elementary things.

The same is true of pure notes in our auditory experience, and of localized sensations of heat or pain.

Of course, such elementary things differ from those of the physical world, since they are more immediately experienced. Yet they share with them something very essential; that is, they cannot be communicated.

We can give an account of our complex images of phenomena. For instance, we can state that the green of this leaf is identical to the green we find at the coordinates 0.3/0.4 on a color chart placed next to it. We thereby communicate a fact about our picture of phenomena. But by any such statement we cannot communicate the phenomenon *green* itself.

The case is the same with any mental experience, such as grief at someone's death. Indeed, with a bit of training in self-observation, we can divide the complex whole of the experience into pieces: enumerating memories of the dead person, our love for her, thoughts of our future loneliness, and so on. But we cannot communicate the grief which colors all these elements.

1.5 Logical Form of Things

Elementary things have no properties in the sense in which we ascribe properties to the ordinary things in the world. Nevertheless, elementary things are not indeterminate.

Every one of them may occur in elementary facts. However, the facts must be of a certain kind. For example, elementary things of the material world can occur in connection with space-time changes such as intensities and forces, but not in connection with mental states. Color, as a phenomenon, can occur in facts within our visual field, such as the color of an object that we see. It can also occur in facts concerning colors as such, like the contrast we feel between a color and its complementary color. But it cannot occur in matters of acoustics.

There are similar limits for complex things to occur in facts. For instance, gravity of physics cannot occur in an intrinsic connection with color blindness.

The possibilities with which things may occur in actual facts are called by Wittgenstein their *formal properties*, or alternately their *internal properties*. This is in contrast with the external properties, which are properties in the true sense.

An internal property is necessary to a thing. The essence of an external property is that a thing may or may not have it. Internal properties can be defined by enumerating the possible ways a thing can occur, but also in some cases by abstract statements.

Thus it is inseparable from objects in space that statements can be made about their position in space. Specifically, for each point within such an object, three numbers can be specified that define the coordinates in an arbitrarily chosen coordinate system.

It is inseparable from colors that they can be arranged according to their degrees of similarity—for example, red, orange, and yellow. All colors can be represented together in a three-dimensional system using tint, degree of darkening, and degree of lightening.

Wittgenstein calls such characteristics of the most general kind, particularly those concerning the compatibility or incompatibility of occurring together, the *logical form* of things. That things will at any given time retain their fixed logical form is the basis of the "logic of the world," a phrase used by Wittgenstein to express the fact that we can find our way about the world by means of logical thinking. This is impossible in the world of feverish dreams, where the logical form of things is blurred.

1.6 Essential Unconnectedness of Facts

As we have seen, it is in the nature of elementary things that they do not occur in isolation—indeed, are connected with one another by means of facts. At first glance, it would appear that some facts we meet in the world may be connected with one another by some conditions.

This interconnection is often merely the chance that several facts concern the same object. Connections of this kind—such as between the two facts "This book has two hundred pages" and "It is written in French"—are fortuitous.

But there are other facts that on the contrary seem to have an internal, necessary connection with one another.

A particular example are facts about events that follow one another in temporal succession and concern two or more objects. An instance is the collision of two billiard balls and the subsequent recoil.

In the case of a temporal connection of this kind, we speak of a causal connection or a cause-and-effect relation between two facts. We also speak of the rule of natural laws by which one event is followed by a foreseeable—indeed, absolutely determined—event, and not just by some arbitrary event.

In daily life, we get along very well by assuming the truth of such causal connections or natural laws. For example, if a pot is put on a fire, can't we predict with certainty that it will get hot? Yet physics objects: Although the passage of heat from a hotter to a colder body is a valid rule for cooking in a kitchen, it is not a strict law of nature. What appears to us as heat, is in physics a disorderly movement of atoms. In a hot body, this movement is *on average* faster than in a cold one. Indeed, when the two bodies touch, the faster moving atoms on average pass some of their energy of motion to the slower ones. But the opposite must also occur in small areas of a body, and indeed is observed to do so.

In fact, the events of the macroscopic world are not determined by strict laws, but rather by extremely reliable rules. For example, according to the rules of gravity, a stone released from some height will always fall down to the ground. But quantum physics declares that there is a probability, though very small, that at some point in time, a stone may rise in the air instead of fall, contrary to the rule of gravity. This exceptional event is predicted to occur once in tens of billions of years.

If perfect strictness existed in natural laws at all, it would be confined to the world of atoms. Even supposing that we found it there, could we mean by it anything other than regularity? Are we entitled to speak of necessity in connection with consecutive facts? That the idea of necessity has for so long been applied unhesitatingly but wrongly to the events of the macroscopic world should be a warning that we must be very careful.

The word "necessary" has a clear meaning in the case of logical necessity, as found for instance in the logical conclusions we draw in a mathematical proof. In that case, we can *know*—in the genuine sense of the word—that something is true if something else is true. Our knowledge of logical necessity is of an a priori nature, not depending upon real experiences. We possess no such knowledge of natural laws.

In Wittgenstein's view, facts are only externally connected by their simultaneous occurrence in a configuration of things, and not by any inner necessity. Although the consecutiveness of two events may invariably have been observed, we still do not know—in the strict meaning of the word—that this will also be the case in the future.

1.6 ESSENTIAL UNCONNECTEDNESS OF FACTS

Wittgenstein's opinion produces less of a shock today than it must have caused in 1921, when his Tractatus first appeared. For in the meantime, physics has further undermined our old ideas of the iron laws of nature. The discovery of the bending phenomena observable in corpuscular radiation has in fact led us to view the sequence of movements occurring on the atomic scale as something determined by rules whose validity is only statistical—that is, as an average of many individual cases—and not absolute.

Such experiences help us understand Wittgenstein's thesis. But we must remember that they can neither prove it nor disprove it. For even if everything, down to the smallest detail, happened exactly according to some supposed law, that, too, would be mere chance according to Wittgenstein.

We can agree to all this, at least in the following sense: We should make sure that we do not take the idea of necessity occurring in logic and apply it to the world of events.

Obviously, the crudely visible facts of the world are fortuitous as well, since they are composed of elementary facts, every one of which is fortuitous.

Wittgenstein expresses the above arguments as follows.

> *It is a hypothesis that the sun will rise tomorrow; and that means that we do not know whether it will rise.* (Tractatus 6.36311)

Just as the observed regularity and relative predictability of natural events make us speak loosely about necessity, so likewise we have been led by the events within our minds—about which nothing can ever be predicted with certainty—to the use of an equally foggy idea: the notion of freedom—in particular, of free will.

What Wittgenstein says about this lies outside the traditional controversies about free will. That battle addressed the following questions: Should the functioning of our motives and decisions be interpreted along the lines of causally connected sequences of events in nature, though in this case we cannot trace in detail the events or their connections? Or are our decisions formed spontaneously, without being forced on us by our motives?

Wittgenstein confines himself to the only point that is clear in the idea of freedom, heavily charged with emotions as it is:

> *The essence of free will is that future actions cannot be known now. We could know them only if causality were an* inner *necessity like that of logical inference.* (Tractatus 5.1362)

Although there are no necessary connections—in the strict sense—among the facts of the world, this is not incompatible with our ability in the natural sciences, especially in physics, to infer a multitude of facts one from another in perfectly logical fashion, often by mathematical considerations.

There are indeed purely logical connections, not of course in nature, but in our description of nature. Actually, we do not infer different facts one from another, but an aspect of a fact from another aspect of the same fact.

For example, consider the fact that disturbances on a still surface of water spread over it in all directions with equal speed. If we conclude that waves on the surface of water form circles around their point of origin, then we have not stumbled upon a new fact. Indeed, we have merely expressed the same fact in another manner.

1.7 Things, the Substance of the World

Wittgenstein's analysis of the world may give the impression that the world is devoid of substance. Indeed, the world seems to be an accumulation of relations and connections except for a sort of sediment called elementary things. These elementary

1.7 THINGS, THE SUBSTANCE OF THE WORLD

things are not part of the world. They have no properties, and we can state nothing about them except the connections in which they occur. Such connections, called facts, are not connected by any inner necessity, but simply by the fact that they either occur together or follow each other. Wittgenstein says:

> *Each item can be the case or not the case while everything else remains the case.* (Tractatus 1.21)

Anyone who finds all this difficult to accept should call to mind once more that we are focusing on the world common to all thinking beings. In everyday life, we too easily delude ourselves about how much is exactly the same for us and our fellow citizens. Wittgenstein demolishes these delusions.

Yet the world has substance, in the sense that there is something beyond mere phantoms that get combined higgledy-piggledy as if in a dream.

That something does not itself belong to the world. It consists precisely of what is *not* our common possession as humans, and *not* of what we can pass on to one another by communication. It consists of elementary things. Wittgenstein calls them *objects*, or depending on context, *things*; see Appendix B. We cannot communicate them, but nevertheless they are the items that provide consistency for our communications.

> *Objects make up the substance of the world.* (Tractatus 2.021)

Even though elementary things are beyond our powers of communication, we surely are aware of them. Wittgenstein expresses this by saying "they manifest themselves."

This is certainly the case for the objects in our consciousness. For instance, the colors we see force themselves upon us. However, it is also true of physical objects, except that these force themselves upon us when our intelligence acts upon our surroundings.

A fixed and substantial feature of elementary things is their unchangeable logical form—the fact that every one of them can only occur together with certain other ones and only in predetermined connections. The logical form of objects can only manifest itself. When we try to state anything about it beyond purely abstract generalities like dimensionality, we regress to tautologies. For example, a spatial object cannot be explained without referring to space.

The next chapter examines the representation of the world by pictures, for example, geographical maps and technical drawings. Specifically, things and facts of the world are tied to picture elements and their relations.

Chapter 2

Communication

2.1 Means of Communication

There are a great many methods for communicating something—that is, passing on information. The methods can be classified into three groups.

The first group of methods uses propositions formulated in words and thus consists of speech and various forms of writing.

Speech includes sign language, where propositions are formed by a succession of gestures.

Writing may use phonetic symbols, syllabic symbols, or hieroglyphs. It may also use figures and other symbols—for example, in the equations used in mathematics and physics, which are propositions written in a kind of shorthand.

For simplified terminology, from now on we will use the term "speech" to mean both oral and written propositions. Thus, the first group of methods is speech in various forms.

The second group of methods includes drawings, photographs, maps whether in relief or plane, solid models of machines for training purposes, and also every kind of information in the form of graphs, such as temperature charts. All these methods rely on our senses, most often of sight.

Both groups have in common that they rely on a composition process that uses many different signs. In the case of speech propositions, the signs are individual words. On a map, they are the signs representing rivers, towns, heights above sea level, and so forth.

Lastly, there are methods of communication where for each bit of information exactly one sign is employed. Examples are exclamations such as "Halt!" or "Fire!", the red traffic light meaning "Stop!", or the blaring sound of a siren. Clearly, the use of these signs and their ability to express anything is limited. Yet they do play an important role in our lives.

In the three means of communication we have named, speech is of overwhelming importance.

The methods of the second group, which mostly rely on our sense of sight, do not by themselves provide any information; we first must explain them in words. Here are two examples.

First, in a graph, the meaning of the coordinates has to be stated.

Second, a photo can only give us information about something unknown when we have been told what the photo represents; the photo itself does not give that preliminary information. For instance, a photo showing palm trees can only tell us something about the composition of southern flora if we are first told that it was taken in a southern landscape and not in some botanical garden.

Once an informational method of the second group has been explained to us, it tells us more than has been included in that explanation. For example, suppose for a map the signs for rivers, roads, railroads, and so on have been explained. Then without further help, the map tells us much about the depicted country.

The isolated symbols in our third group are not like this. They just say what has already been explained to us, and no more. To understand them, we first must have learned their whole message. For example, we learned as children that, when a building is burning, a shout of "Fire!" is a cry for help and not a request for a match to light a cigarette. Consequently, the signs in the third group are rarely used to make statements, but rather as signals or instructions to behave or act in a certain way.

We can therefore confine our inquiry into means of communication to the two first two groups, which rely on a composition process that involves many symbols.

It must be emphasized—and this is of decisive importance for understanding the Tractatus—that in the case of speech we are only interested in speech propositions that are intended to actually convey information. Typically, this is not the case with lyric poems, songs, requests, prayers, or curses.

2.2 Wittgenstein's Picture Theory

We have already seen that the informational methods we are concerned with have a common feature: They assemble signs to convey information. How do they manage to do that?

In the Tractatus, Wittgenstein develops a theory of language–today called *picture theory*—that supplies the following answer: The *propositions*—the logicians' name for statements—*that occur in speech are pictures of the reality that is to be conveyed.*

In everyday speech, making a picture of an object means producing something that has—or at least is intended to have—an obvious resemblance to the object. We call the product a representation of the object, or a picture of it.

In daily life, "picture" has a slightly less precise sense than "representation" and often is used in a metaphorical sense. Wittgenstein uses both words in the same sense. But what is the exact meaning in his picture theory?

The question is easily answered for the informational methods of the second group. Here, "representation" typically is interpreted directly depending on the method. For example, it refers to a photograph, or a drawing of things, or a map. As an exception, the temperature chart of a patient may in everyday usage be referred to more vaguely as a picture of the course of fever, but rarely as a representation.

For speech propositions—our first group of means of communication—the word "representation" is rather unusual. Only in special cases do we call a proposition a picture or representation. For example, the picture case occurs when a proposition employs a simile, such as saying "the storm is dying down" when a dispute is becoming less intense.

Wittgenstein calls not only such propositions but *all* informational propositions *pictures* or *representations*. Obviously, that use relies on a more general idea than the everyday notion of a representation.

2.3 Wittgenstein's Idea of a Picture

Let us take a look at the diagram of connections of a radio. The drawing obviously belongs to the second group of informational methods. On the diagram, we find symbols for switches, transistors, coils, etc., and a number of lines indicating electrical connections between these constructional elements.

The symbols of the constructional elements in no way resemble the actual elements, nor does their position in the diagram correspond to their position in the actual radio. Also, the connecting lines between the symbols take a different course, bend at different places, and cross one another in different ways than the actual wires in the set.

There is only one point where the diagram of connections agrees with reality; it shows how parts are connected by wires. For the technician making the connections, the diagram is a good picture of the radio. It doesn't matter at all that most of the diagram does not resemble reality.

2.3 Wittgenstein's Idea of a Picture

Things that are pictures only in this broader sense are called *models of reality*. A model does not have to reproduce every characteristic of the reality it represents, whether the reality is a thing or a process. It only must have the characteristics needed at a given moment.

The model of an engine intended only for instruction may well have pistons made of wood, but it must clearly show at which positions of the pistons the valves are open or closed.

Wittgenstein's idea of a picture is a bit more abstract. In his view, the following two conditions are sufficient to characterize a picture:

(1) Its elements, called the *picture elements*, must represent things in the reality which is being pictured.
(2) The relations existing between the picture elements must represent relations between the real things in such a way that the latter relations can be read off, so to speak.

We illustrate the idea of a picture with an example used by Wittgenstein: the sketch of a house. The drawing contains an element in the form of a quadrangle that represents the roof. Another element is in the form of a coat of red coloring matter that represents redness visible on the real house. Moreover, a relation exists in the picture between these two elements. That is, the coat of red coloring material just covers the quadrangle. From this relation in the picture, we read off the fact that the roof of the actual house has something to do with redness.

The sketch would not be a picture at all—in the sense that we are discussing—if the elements standing for the roof and redness were not arranged so as to indicate their connection—for instance, if the red was put just somewhere at the edge of the picture, as can occur in modern paintings.

The elements in the sketch of the house and those of the real house have a visible resemblance. Due to this fact, the example is too narrow to serve as a generally valid explanation of the picture idea.

Fundamentally, such a resemblance is not necessary. The real redness of the roof could have been equally well represented by a particular kind of hatching having a pre-agreed meaning, as is the custom in heraldry.

Indeed, picture elements can be very different from the real elements they represent. A piece of music can be depicted in a score, the sounds being represented by the notation, or on a vinyl record using wave impressions in the grooves as picture elements.

The picture elements must obey the following three conditions.

First, the picture must contain as many different kinds of elements as there are different real elements that are to be distinguished.

Second, each picture element must always represent the same kind of real element.

The third condition is a bit more complicated. Although the elements of the picture and their arrangement need not have any obvious resemblance to reality, something in the picture and the real object must in some sense be not merely similar, but absolutely identical. Specifically, between the picture elements, the same number of kinds of relations must be possible, the same number be necessary, and the same number be incompatible as between the corresponding elements of reality. In other words, the relations between the elements in the reality and those between the elements in the picture must exhibit the *same mathematical multiplicity*.

When the three conditions are satisfied, Wittgenstein says that picture and reality have *identical structure*.

The requirement of identical structure is met automatically when the picture elements and the real elements are of the

2.3 Wittgenstein's Idea of a Picture

same nature—for instance, when real colors are to be depicted by colors in the picture, degrees of brightness by degrees of brightness, and spatial elements by spatial elements.

But the requirement of identical structure becomes something quite out of the ordinary when the elements of reality are to be represented by pictorial elements of a different type. Let us look at a few examples.

The colors humans perceive can be classified according to three kinds of relations. First, by their hue—for example red, blue, or green. Second, by their white content—for example red, pink, or bright pink. Third, by their black content—for example red, reddish brown, or dark reddish brown.

When we combine white content and black content to one measure, we see that the color relations are of twofold multiplicity. This approach is used in the *color wheel*. As soon as we have that arrangement, we can determine each color by its geometric position in the wheel.

A piece of music, for the purpose of making a picture of it on a vinyl record, is a temporal sequence of sounds. Each sound contains notes of varying pitch. Each note has its proper degree of strength. For stereo recordings, the two sound channels are recorded by the waveform of the two sides of the V groove.

The next two examples examine presence or absence of identity of structure, stated before as follows: If relations of a particular kind are possible, necessary, or incompatible among the particular elements of the reality to be depicted, then an equal number of possible, necessary, or incompatible relations must appear between the picture elements.

An example of such agreement involves the plane and the sphere, as taught in geography: One can depict on the plane the surface of a sphere with the exception of a single point of the sphere. For one possible construction, imagine a globe model resting with its south pole on the plane. For any point of the globe except the north pole, draw the line going through that point and the north pole. The intersection of the line with the plane is a point in the plane corresponding to the point on the sphere. Clearly, each point on the globe can be so processed except the north pole.

An example of disagreement involves the plane and the torus; that is, one cannot make a flat picture of a torus. For between the elements of the surface of a torus, there are possible relations to which nothing on a flat surface corresponds. For a demonstration, define a *simple closed curve* on a surface to be a connected curve that does not cross itself and ends at the same point where it begins. Every such curve divides the plane into two separate regions, the inner region and the outer region. But on the torus there are curves that do not divide up the surface at all; for example, the largest circle on the torus.

We see now that what makes a picture a picture is not any particular choice of elements, such as choosing them for their resemblance to the real elements. Indeed, the picture elements can be quite different. But essential are the relations and connections between the picture elements. Wittgenstein calls these relations and connections *facts*.

Suppose in a given picture a variety of facts occur simultaneously. Then this simultaneous occurrence is also a fact. It informs us that in the depicted reality there is also a corresponding set of facts occurring together. In this sense, the following is true of the picture as a whole:

A picture is a fact. (Tractatus 2.141)

2.4 True and False Pictures

Identity of structure in picture and reality, in the sense explained above, is not enough to guarantee the truth of a picture, but only to make it a picture at all. It may still be true or false.

For example, the sketch of the house mentioned earlier would be a false picture if the real roof was not red but black. The truth of a picture can only be ascertained by comparison with reality, and not by just looking at the picture.

Even a false picture is still a picture, and not just something meaningless. For the sketch in our example to be a picture of the house, it is not necessary for the facts depicted in the picture to exist in reality; they need only be possible. Identity of structure guarantees that this is the case.

Now assume identity of structure. Then a picture is *true* if the following two conditions are satisfied.

First, as many elements must be distinguishable in the picture as are needed to describe the house. The extent of the need depends on the situation. For example, an architect will require other elements in the house than a house painter.

Second, the relations between the picture elements must be clearly associated with the relations existing between the elements of the real house—as we explained when dealing with the relation between the roof and the color of the roof.

If this second requirement is met, but the picture contains fewer elements than reality and therefore also fewer relations (facts), then it will not be called false but *incomplete*. For example, if our sketch shows no chimney, an architect would consider the picture incomplete.

2.5 Logical Form Common to Picture and Reality

In Chapter 1 we spoke of the formal or internal properties of both elementary and complex things. We meant by this the variety of determining characteristics we need to know about a thing: How it can occur in facts in conjunction with other things, and the various relations of compatibility or incompatibility it can have with them.

We also defined the totality of a thing's internal properties as its logical form.

We now have encountered the same determining characteristics in our inquiry into pictures. Every picture—whether true or false—must have in common with the depicted object the degree of multiplicity of its elements and of the relations possible between them.

In addition, if it is to be a true picture, then the relations between its elements must reflect the relations which exist in reality. Therefore, we can say that every picture must have in common with its object at least its *logical form*. Or as Wittgenstein puts it:

> *Every picture is* also *a logical one.* (Tractatus 2.182)

The word "also" implies that a picture can in addition have more specialized qualities, such as being spatial or colored.

2.6 Form of Representation

It is not obvious from a picture which things are represented by which elements in the picture, nor which kinds of relations between real things are reproduced by which kinds of relations between picture elements. This information must be found outside the picture.

For example, in a map the meaning of its colors needs explanation. On some maps, green areas represent wooded country, but on others, lowlands. The explanations of colors, hatchings, and other symbols are not sufficient for us to deduce from the spatial relations on the map the real relations of position and distance. For this, we need to know the scale of the map.

The manner in which the relations in the picture reflect the real relations is called by Wittgenstein the *form of representation*.

2.7 Thoughts and Speech Propositions

Recall that Section 2.5 leads up to the following conclusion:

Every picture is also *a logical one.* (Tractatus 2.182)

The theory goes on to say that there are *purely* logical pictures defined as follows:

First, they do not require any material means of representation.

Second, they do not have any perceptible likeness to, or characteristic shared with, the pictured object, except the indispensable sharing of its logical form.

These pictures represent not only our thoughts, but also the speech propositions by which our thoughts are transmitted to others. Wittgenstein states this as follows:

A logical picture of facts is a thought. (Tractatus 3)

In a proposition, a thought finds an expression that can be perceived by the senses. (Tractatus 3.1)

The word *thought* as used above requires more precise explanation. As is customary among philosophers, Wittgenstein makes a distinction between thoughts and the mental events of thinking, in which mental images of things and of words occur within us.

As an example, suppose we think "France is larger than Belgium." At the same time, we can imagine ourself accommodating on a map the whole area of Belgium well inside France.

The thought is not identical with this act of imagination, any more than the number 5 is identical with our imagination of five apples.

Thus, the thought is something abstracted from the images; it emerges from them. Our ability to examine a thought, to consider it, and to discuss it with other people—as if it were something effectively present—arises from our ability to make perceptible images. The component parts of the images—for example, Belgium and France on the map—then represent the component parts of the thought.

We make up signs for the components of the thought, and for the thought itself. In practice, we use for this purpose the words and propositions of speech.

In principle, other kinds of elements could be used for this purpose. As Wittgenstein remarks, signs used for the thought might be

> *... composed of spatial objects (such as tables, chairs, and books) instead of written signs.*
> *Then the spatial arrangement of these things will express the sense of the proposition.* (Tractatus 3.1431)

There has been controversy as to whether we can think without formulating verbal propositions in our minds. That is a psychological question of no importance for the present inquiry, for we are not discussing the *process* of thought.

The essential thing is that we are *able* to express our thoughts in words. We often have the experience of curious thoughts that we are not able to put into words—for instance, what we take for thoughts in a dream—and that upon closer consideration turn out to be simple chains of associations.

Since thoughts become intelligible only by being expressed in propositions, could not the picture theory have been more simply formulated, without mentioning thoughts at all, by saying that *propositions* are logical pictures of facts?

Indeed, if a picture of an object, such as the sketch of a house, is itself pictured over again, say by photographing it, the result is, after all, just another picture of the object.

So why explain the picture theory in a roundabout way by introducing thoughts, which constitute an interim picture that does not even really exist?

The reason is this: In verbal propositions, as in all material means of expression, many variations are possible. Indeed, the propositions are formed using spoken words according to grammatical rules. Both the words and the rules of grammar allow a certain freedom to express the same thought in various ways. Instead of saying "France is larger than Belgium," we can say "Belgium is smaller than France," expressing thereby the same thought.

Now as far as our inquiry into the nature of communication is concerned, we are only marginally interested in propositions as grammatical formations. Indeed, we want to know what it is in the propositions that is *not* an accidental variation. And that consists precisely of the thoughts that propositions express.

Having thus clarified our ideas, we shall feel free from now on to proceed as follows. Whenever Wittgenstein does not explicitly speak of propositions as actual strings of words, we interpret the word "proposition" to mean not the grammatical construction but the logical one—that is, the relation between ideas.

Similarly, "word" does not mean—unless the contrary is stated—the combination of letters but the idea for which it stands. Of course, the inquiry must be carried out by some concrete means—that is, by verbally formulated propositions. But we shall not cling too closely to their grammatical exterior.

2.8 Elements and Structure of Verbal Pictures

If the picture theory is to be anything more than a vague allegory, one must be able to demonstrate the following.

First, that the objects of reality are represented by the elements of the propositions—that is, by its words.

Second, that the relations between things, which constitute the facts of reality, are represented by the way the words in the proposition are related to one another—that is, by the structure of the proposition.

In an inflected language such as German, the structure of a proposition includes not only the order of the words and the way they are grouped by punctuation, but also the case endings that imply relations between words in the proposition.

Structure is also expressed by many things that are words in the grammatical sense, but are meaningless outside a proposition.

For instance, take the word "is." It can be used as a simple link, as in the proposition "the leaf is green." But elsewhere it can have a meaning of its own, such as "exists" or "is equal to." The same is true of the word "has" in propositions like "the equation has two solutions," where it asserts a particular connection between two ideas and does not mean "possesses."

Not only in verbal pictures but in other kinds as well, elements are sometimes used that strictly speaking are not picture elements. Indeed, they do not represent real things, but only indicate related information. For instance, a technical drawing of a machine contains dotted lines which show how horizontal and vertical sections correspond. Similarly, two-way arrows indicate measurements.

The picture theory directly concerns only simple propositions that do not contain negations. We shall see later how the theory deals with propositions containing negations such as "not" or "none," and with complex propositions where component propositions are logically bound together by "if," "or," "and," and so on.

Just using the insight gained so far into the elements and structure of propositions, many simple propositions can without further ado be explained as pictures. In the simple proposition "The book is on the writing pad," the words "book" and "writing pad" represent real things; that is, they are names.

Then "is on" denotes a spatial relation, which in the logical form is also a thing. The structure of the proposition consists of the fact that the two names "book" and "writing pad" are separated by the name of the relation, and "book" comes first and "writing pad" after the relation.

The meaning of "is on" is that the name coming before it denotes the higher placed object, and the name coming after it the lower placed one. Thus, the fact that the words are ordered in a certain way allows us to express a fact in space.

2.9 Elementary Propositions

The picture theory does not claim that all simple propositions—in the casual form in which we meet them in daily speech—can at once be identified as pictures of reality. It asserts rather that the underlying thoughts *can* be expressed in propositions which are pictures in the sense we have explained.

Indeed, the propositions occurring in everyday language often include elements that aren't part of the actual information. Examples are words expressing wishes, beliefs, or doubts of the speaker, like "I hope" and "regrettably"; or words intended to draw the attention of the listener to some important point, like the word "himself" in the proposition "he saw it himself."

More importantly, colloquial propositions contain adjectives, and these are neither names of things, nor do they serve to assert relations between the names occurring in the proposition. They are, in fact, names of properties.

In Chapter 1 we explained that properties only occur in things that are complex. For by analytical description, we can arrive at simpler things, and finally at elementary things, and these have no properties.

Hence, we can process a proposition of everyday language containing adjectives—that is, property names—as follows. We replace every combination of name-plus-adjective by a description of the complex thing to which the combination refers. Then we do the same with the resulting names-plus-adjectives, and so on, until there are only elementary things. At that time, we have obtained from the original proposition a series of propositions in which property names no longer occur.

Propositions about elementary things can only state facts. Wittgenstein calls such propositions *elementary propositions*, and he calls the process which leads us from an ordinary proposition to elementary ones the *analysis* of the ordinary proposition.

In suitable context, he often calls elementary propositions simply *propositions*.

At last, we see that—in the strict meaning of the picture theory—elementary propositions are pictures of real facts. They contain only names of things—indeed, of elementary things—and the order of the names can then depict the relations between these things. In this connection, we must remember that among elementary things we also find incorporeal items such as elementary space relations and elementary time events.

We have already pointed out that an analysis of the complex things in the world right down to elementary things is impossible. This implies that it is also impossible to carry out a complete analysis of everyday propositions.

How far we can push the analysis obviously depends upon our perseverance, our detailed knowledge, and our ability to keep in mind the ever increasing network of new propositions that we discover.

A very useful model, which helps us to understand such an analysis, is the method for preparing a patent claim for a complicated machine.

The initial simple description mentions only the principal components of the machine. Then the naming of these components is replaced by enumeration of their sub-components, their relative positions, and their interconnections. The same procedure is then applied to the sub-components, and so on. The process stops when in the entire description the named parts are so simple that a specialist can no longer have any misunderstanding about the characteristics of the machine.

The example of a patent claim is not only a useful elucidation of how analysis works. It also explains why Wittgenstein attached such importance to the reducibility of propositions to elementary propositions. In his view, the reducibility gives our communications precise meaning.

Indeed, many propositions that deal with complex things contain something indeterminate. The propositions of daily speech do this more than any others. In the Dialogues of Plato, Socrates is constantly obliged to ask his interlocutors "What do you mean by that?" This question comes to an end when elementary propositions are reached.

Just as the world common to all men consists of the totality of facts, so must all possible communications about the world be capable of being assembled out of the totality of valid elementary propositions. This is true for communications concerning individual events and relations—as in daily life and in history—and likewise for communications of general import arising from empirical science. Wittgenstein calls this totality natural science. However, he includes psychology.

> *The totality of true propositions is the whole of natural science (or the whole corpus of the natural sciences).* (Tractatus 4.11)

2.10 Precise Definition of the Tractatus Problem

Up to this point, the problem of the nature of communication addressed in the Tractatus was defined by the following three, rather vague, questions introduced in Chapter 1:

First, how is information passed on?
Second, what conditions must our speech comply with so that genuine information is transferred?
Third, what can be so conveyed?

We now can make these questions precise.

First, what is essential in a speech proposition?
Second, what distinguishes a meaningful proposition from a mere string of words?
Third, what can we communicate by a proposition?

The remainder of this section begins to address these questions and covers related issues. The next chapter includes the answers given by the Tractatus.

The first question—how is information passed on?—is answered by Wittgenstein's picture theory. Nevertheless, some questions remain open regarding the kinds of representation that are characteristic of propositions.

For an answer of the second question—what conditions must our speech comply with so that genuine information is transferred?—we must start from the already adopted view that the arrangement of words in a meaningful proposition must express relations between real things.

Now words can be arranged so that they do nothing of the kind; many surrealist poems are examples. Therefore, we must inquire what arrangements of what kind of words furnish pictures. For a start, we should look for guiding principles derived from the very idea of representation.

The third question—what can we communicate by a proposition?—obviously has the greatest philosophical importance.

We already know that propositions can communicate facts. In particular, we have seen that hidden communications concerning elementary facts occur in every proposition.

2.11 Value of Picture Theory

The elementary propositions, which explicitly communicate these elementary facts, cannot always—and maybe cannot ever—be isolated in the pure state. But by pushing the analysis far enough, we can always reach things and propositions that are elementary enough for the practical circumstances of any particular case.

However, the following question arises: Can propositions and complex propositions of everyday speech communicate something more than the facts discovered during the analysis?

Let us rephrase the question. Suppose we turn simple propositions—that is, our hypothetical elementary propositions or any other propositions that communicate nothing but facts—into propositions of daily speech. The process may apply artifices of style to the simple propositions and may introduce negation into them. But above all, it creates propositions with sentence structure. What meanings can the resulting propositions of daily speech have?

Suppose the answer is that propositions of daily speech can express nothing but facts. This would imply that our thoughts, insofar as they are real thoughts capable of being communicated, can only occur within the sphere of facts. Or as many of us would say with regret, on a dull level of matter-of-factness.

Put differently, whenever we think, we make for ourselves a picture of a factual situation, in the strict sense explained on the preceding pages. Does this still permit a higher flight of the intellect? Is it still possible for us to wrestle in thought with questions that concern us more deeply than facts, such as the quest of the meaning of life and of the world, and about moral values? Such thoughts should not, indeed must not, depend on what actually is occurring in the world.

In view of these weighty consequences, it is fitting that we insert here a retrospective summary and evaluation of the picture theory.

2.11 Intellectual Value of the Picture Theory

If we had to pass on information with isolated signs such as single words and not with propositions, we would need as many signs as we had pieces of information to communicate. In a primitive tribe with a very limited and unvarying cycle of occurrences, such a method of communication might be conceivable. But every time there was something new to communicate, a new sign would have to be introduced and explained by a reference to the new event.

On the other hand, if one wants to communicate new events with a limited number of signs, the only possible way is to arrange the signs in groups. It is not immediately obvious how this can be done in such a way that one can communicate every new event intelligibly without having to explain the groups of signs.

For instance, it is not self-evident—as the picture theory maintains—that things are represented by words and the relations between the things by the way the words are arranged. Why couldn't words also specify relations?

From this detail, we see already that the picture theory is not a statement that is a priori true; nor can this be demonstrated.

If we consider our own speech propositions, we are forced to admit that the theory states something that is correct. But we would like to say something about speech that isn't just empirical.

For an evaluation of the picture theory, it is relevant that we feel an overall mental discomfort in trying to state in words and propositions what words and proposition are. The concept of representation of the picture theory provides insight into the source of our discomfort.

According to the arguments in Section 2.6 concerning the form of representation, a picture conveys no information about the

2.11 Value of Picture Theory

form in which it represents reality. In pictures not produced by speech this creates no problem. For example, in a map a table can be added in the margin that explains the signs employed.

But in a purely logical picture, and in its reflection in speech, we do not have at our disposal a margin, so to speak, that lies outside the language used.

Indeed, the propositions which we would need for an explanation are themselves parts of language.

> *Propositions can exhibit the whole of reality, but they cannot exhibit what they must have in common with reality in order to represent it—logical form.*
> *In order to be able to represent logical form, we should have to be able to station ourselves with propositions somewhere outside logic, that is to say outside the world.* (Tractatus 4.12)

This holds not just for any proposition with its particular form of representation, but for speech as a whole.

In his picture theory, Wittgenstein attempts to say about propositions exactly how much can possibly be said in language. He first explains to us what a representation consists of, by pointing out the characteristics common to all representations.

Then he confronts us with speech propositions and asks, as it were, whether anything attracts our attention. What we are expected to notice cannot be explained by a process of demonstration; it can only appear to us.

We must see this for ourselves, just as we have to see for ourselves what the difference is between red and green. One can only give hints that may help us to see more clearly.

Such hints are sometimes needed in daily life. Not everyone can spot game in a thicket, or fish beneath smooth water, but a hunter or a fisherman can make us see them. Such directions for seeing are contained in Wittgenstein's explanations of what can be communicated about the world, especially in his thesis that everything communicable that we find in the world can be reduced to facts.

Hints about something that we can only see for ourselves will not strike everyone as being a sufficient point for an intellectual construction. After all, even actual vision contains possibilities of error. Yet, if we are to philosophize, this is something we must accept.

Toward the end of this book, we will return to the above concerns and discuss them in detail.

The next chapter shows that every thought—as well as the corresponding proposition of language—is a combination of pictures, each of which depicts parts of the world, that is, things and facts.

Chapter 3

Efficiency of Speech

It isn't easy to describe the main lines along which Wittgenstein pursues his inquiry into the logical nature of simple and complex propositions. While doing so, he also works out the requirements for a meaningful proposition and what propositions can say in principle.

His inquiries do not rest exclusively on the concepts of the communicable world and of the way in which communications about it are made using pictures—topics that have occupied us till now.

On the contrary, as one of the founders of modern logic, he also develops a number of related logical theses. In fact, his purely logical reflections frequently outgrow the limits of an inquiry into the efficiency of speech.

Sometimes, even professional philosophers do not entirely succeed in giving a methodical account of the very abstract train of thought in this part of the Tractatus. A partial reason for this are Wittgenstein's all too brief statements, which at times resemble aphorisms.

Some of the material reflects disagreement with other logicians, like Gottlob Frege and Bertrand Russell; related brief notes of Wittgenstein, recorded before the Tractatus as well as subsequently, barely succeed in clarifying even the core of the problems under discussion.

As a result, we are forced to confine ourselves to discussion of some of Wittgenstein's essential ideas and conclusions. In the rather loose form in which they are set out here, without the aid of his notation for logic, they indeed do not describe the results of his book. But they familiarize us with his method of inquiry and help us grasp the meaning of its central results.

3.1 Peculiarities of Picture Components

Let us first consider the raw material available in speech for making pictures.

The components of a proposition that contribute to its meaning from a logical, not grammatical, viewpoint, are called *symbols* by Wittgenstein. The perceptible portions of the symbols—for example, nouns, adjectives and so on, but also whole portions of the proposition—are called the *signs* of the symbols.

If we treat the symbols as identical with the signs, fatal errors will arise, in particular because a single word can be the sign of different symbols. For instance, the word "is" may occur as a simple link—without any separate meaning of its own—or as the sign of equality, or with the meaning "exists."

The essence of a symbol is not its sign, but the way in which the sign is used. When we say in the picture theory that the words of a proposition are the elements of a picture, then by "words" we mean symbols and not signs used for them.

When we discussed the picture, we spoke of the necessity that the elements of the picture and the possible relations between them should exhibit the same degree of multiplicity as exists in elements of the thing to be depicted and in the relations between those elements.

In a proposition, the symbols must reflect the degree of multiplicity of what is symbolized. For example, a proposition intended to communicate something about two persons must use two names—whether proper names or any other means of distinguishing them—and the structure of the proposition must establish a relation between the two names. Similarly, a proposition about a surface must confine itself to concepts of surface—for example, area—and must not contain ideas belonging to a different dimension such as thickness or weight.

3.1 Peculiarities of Picture Components

If we are making a spatial picture of a spatial object—like the teaching model of an engine already mentioned—then we can fit together every spatial element of the picture with every other one. The resulting picture can at most be a false one; in that case, it is the picture of something that perhaps does not exist, but could exist.

When we are making a picture with speech elements, worse can happen. Indeed, we may choose an arbitrary arrangement of speech elements that cannot be a picture of anything.

Hence, the meaningful employment of the words of any language is controlled by the *syntax* of that language. The syntax is made up of rules that define the sole combinations in which a word occurring in a proposition can have any meaning.

An adjective such as "yellow" must be used differently than a correlating word or a phrase like "to the right of": "That flower *is* yellow" versus "That fork *lies* to the right of the plate."

Word sequences having the appearance of propositions, but with false syntax, are occasionally used by advertisers; for example, "Product X is better." This conveys no specific information and is merely meant to stimulate demand for product X.

Why does language need syntax, while other forms of representation—for example, musical notations and maps—manage without anything of the kind? A map can indeed falsely represent Paris to be north of London. But why does language go further than this and make it possible to say something completely nonsensical about the geographical situation of Paris? For example, "Paris is north of sea level."

Nonsense cannot occur if the pictorial elements are so chosen in advance that they possess the same logical form as the elements of the object being depicted. That is, relations between them are mutually compatible or incompatible in agreement with the corresponding cases between the elements of reality.

However, speech elements do not guarantee this, since there are more possible combinations of signs in speech than situations that could possibly occur. Only the restrictive effect of syntax achieves agreement between the combinations of picture elements versus those of real elements.

The various languages of everyday speech have evolved to facilitate daily life rather than make communications as precise as possible. This explains not only the often misleading way in which the signs of everyday speech are employed, but also the high degree of arbitrariness in its syntax. Even the language of science is not exempt from these imperfections.

For these reasons, logicians use an artificial language. Its syntax is purely logical and not empirically formed. In fact, in the language of logic the rules of syntax are self-evident. Consequently, the signs for basic ideas like "not," "all," "if ... then," "thing," and "there is" can no longer cause confusion through some chance similarity in the signs or in the way they are used.

For example, a proposition like "all is transitory" is correctly formed by the standard of colloquial syntax. But it cannot be expressed in the language of logicians, where "all" may only be used when a universe of discourse has been defined.

3.2 Simple Propositions

We define *simple propositions* to be propositions that cannot be analyzed into partial propositions like the condition and conclusion of "if ... then ..." statements. The simple propositions discussed in this section may be propositions in everyday speech. That is, when logically analyzed, they may turn out to be reducible, in contrast to elementary propositions.

Simple propositions fall mostly into the following two groups.

First, propositions saying something about an object, such as "This paper is white," "Lilac smells sweet," or "Whales are aquatic mammals."

Second, propositions expressing the existence of a proportion or relation between two or more objects, such as "This book is thicker than that one," or "Max is Karl's son."

When a simple proposition is considered as a logical picture, then the meaning of the proposition is determined by its components, which we have called symbols. These are solely names of objects, properties, or relations, to the exclusion of logical expressions such as "or," "if ... then ...," and "neither ... nor ...."

Names refer to elements that are part of the reality to be exhibited in the proposition; they represent it in the proposition. This reference or representation is their only task. It completes what we call their *meaning*. But no information is to be found in them. Only the proposition as a whole has a *sense*; it expresses a *thought*.

The above statements are by no means superfluous in view of the ineradicable but superstitious belief that merely naming an object can be true or false, and that just calling something by a name is a meaningful utterance. For example, pantheists think they have said something by calling the universe "God" or "God's body."

Similarly, the proposition as a whole is also a symbol. The sign of this symbol is the spoken or written proposition, which we therefore call the *propositional sign*. Yet the propositional sign is not merely the totality of the elements used in it—namely the words; it consists rather in the fact that these elements are arranged in a particular manner.

Consequently, in Wittgenstein's terminology the propositional sign is a *fact*. If we compare it with marine signals composed of flags, then the point of comparison is not the totality of the flags hoisted in the course of the signal, but the fact that these flags have actually been hoisted in a particular order.

Because the propositional sign is a fact, it can picture other facts, but not objects.

> *Propositions can only say* how *things are, not* what *they are.* (Tractatus 3.221)

In order to understand a proposition, one must have learned the words used and the syntactical rules for using them. But one does not learn beforehand the meaning of the proposition; the proposition is not a name for a fact or for a situation, as we may say of exclamations consisting of single words, like "Attention!" Instead, a proposition can communicate hitherto unknown facts by means of known names. The meaning of a proposition *appears*—is read off, we might say—from the way the words are ordered. For example, if we know the expression "taller than" to be the name of a certain size relation and also know the syntactical rule for grouping the names of the things being compared on either side of this expression, then we can understand the propositions "Paul is taller than Peter" and "Peter is taller than Paul."

So propositions do not themselves tell us how to understand them, or how the facts contained in them depict the facts of reality, any more than a letter entirely written in code can directly communicate the code employed. In particular, a proposition gives no information about the logical form that is common to the real fact and the picture of it.

> *Propositions cannot represent logical form: it is mirrored in them.*
> *What finds its reflection in language, language cannot represent.*
> *What expresses* itself *in language, we cannot express by means of language.*
> *Propositions* show *the logical form of reality.*
> *They display it.* (Tractatus 4.121)
>
> *What* can *be shown,* cannot *be said.* (Tractatus 4.1212)

We can distinguish two parts in the content of a simple proposition:

> *A proposition* shows *its sense.*
> *A proposition* shows *how things stand* if *it is true. And it* says that *they do so stand.* (Tractatus 4.022)

One may say that a proposition gives a picture and asserts that it is a correct one. The assertion of correctness is usually contained in the proposition just by implication, but it can also be added explicitly to the proposition—for example, in a phrase like "It is true that ... ."

Yet neither the picture given by the proposition, nor the assertion that it is a true picture, makes us aware whether the proposition *is* true. To know whether it is true or false, we must compare it with reality. The proposition by itself cannot tell us this.

Therefore, we must require of any meaningful proposition that it be capable of comparison with reality. For a proposition of which it can never be known whether or not it is true, can just as well remain unspoken. *A proposition must enable us to decide how reality appears if it is true, and how reality appears if it is not true.*

This is the *principle of verifiability*, the importance of which—and its applications in science—were later worked out by the philosophers of the Vienna Circle. According to this principle, understanding the sense of a proposition can only mean knowing how things stand if the proposition is true, and how they stand if it is false. This also implies that a proposition only has a meaning if it could also be false. We shall return to this requirement later on. But first we see that the evaluation of a meaningful sentence as true or false may depend on who makes the decision.

For a long time, people considered statements about absolute simultaneity of two events to have a meaning. According to the principle of verifiability, this is so, since an observer essentially could confirm that two events occurred simultaneously.

In everyday life, an accurate enough verification is also possible for events occurring at a distance from each other using communication and synchronized clocks.

Based on this view, people became used to the idea that statements about simultaneity, and more generally about consecutiveness in time, could be true or false, but never without a meaning. Indeed, time was considered as something objective, rather like a fluid evenly permeating the universe.

Even in physics, this belief prevailed until about the turn of the 20th century. At that time, it was found that, under the traditional view, two fundamental experimental results could not be reconciled. This led to Albert Einstein's complete abandonment of the idea of absolute time in his theory of relativity.

Since then it is current practice of physicists to consider statements about time relations of events as only having a meaning if the method of ascertaining the relations is included in the statement.

For example, if two events occur in places that are in different states of motion or rest with respect to the observer—and this is very often the case—then the resulting statement about their order in time can differ according to the position of the observer for which it is intended to be valid. For instance, whether he is at rest with respect to one or other of the places where the two events are occurring; details are included in Appendix A.

The above conclusions—it cannot be seen whether a proposition is true by just examining it, and a proposition has sense only if it could possibly be false—imply that we definitely do not include tautologies or contradictions among genuine propositions. For the truth of tautologies and the falsity of contradictions is a priori assured—that is, without comparison with reality.

3.2 Simple Propositions

It may seem that daily life tautologies such as "Boys will be boys" and "Time passes," and contradictions like "That is true and also not true" and "Sixty minutes are more than an hour" do have a certain meaning or even profundity. But this is only so, because we do not interpret them literally.

Wittgenstein calls tautologies and contradictions *senseless*. We will avoid this term since it could be confused with the term "nonsensical." Instead, since tautologies and contradictions have no meaning, we will use the term "meaningless."

Wittgenstein has to defend application of his term "senseless" to tautologies and contradictions, since they can be extremely valuable. Indeed, arguing back from propositions to tautologies or contradictions is a useful method of proof.

Even the laws of logic and those of mathematics are tautologies. Mathematical laws are arrived at by starting from axioms. Axioms contain no information, and laws are built up by the repeated use of tautologies. For example, there is the procedure of forming new equations by performing the same mathematical operation on both sides of an initial equation.

Seen this way, mathematical propositions tell nothing new—one even is tempted to say that they existed already before they were proved via tautologies. But this conclusion ignores the creative aspect of mathematical constructions—as described, for example, in I. Lakatos's *Proofs and Refutations*.

Tautologies and contradictions are not pictures of reality. They represent no facts. They bring together in a single statement not the names of different things, but only different names of the same things. Thus in the tautology "Time passes," time is first named by the word "time" and second as that which passes.

Tautologies and contradictions have only the *semblance* of propositions. Yet, although they are devoid of meaning and not real propositions, this does not make them nonsense. Wittgenstein reserves the designation "nonsensical" for word pictures that combine the names of things whose logical forms do not fit each other, and thus can be neither true nor false.

Wittgenstein gives us an excellent example:

$2 + 2$ *at* 3 *o'clock equals* 4. (Tractatus 4.1272)

The proposition combines the logical operation $2+2 = 4$, which does not allow spatial or temporal limitation, with an indication of time.

Actually, there is no need to make up artificial examples of this kind. Articles dealing with technical and scientific subjects are full of them. When a storm snapped the antenna of a radio transmitter in two, one article offered this explanation: "The center of gravity of the antenna had broken in two."

Likewise, all propositions are nonsensical that assert the truth of something necessary. They contain no information; for a piece of information tells us something precisely because, instead of its content, something else could have been the case. Consequently, it means nothing if a statement says that the laws of logic are valid.

However, statements about natural processes are not meaningless. For we saw in Chapter 1 the following. Even though the natural processes seem to occur according to some rules, it is not really necessary that they should do so.

Thus, natural laws can be asserted with the interpretation that they describe regularly occurring events. The philosophers who first asserted that the regularity of nature was complete and without exception were in fact going against general opinion, which held that natural events were permeated by chance.

The next page summarizes the definitions of the terms "meaningful," "meaningless" and "nonsensical" as applied to propositions. A new term is "pseudoproposition," which covers the case of a meaningless or nonsensical proposition.

Propositions
1. *Meaningful Propositions*: convey information, may be true or false
2. *Pseudopropositions*: convey no information
   2.1 *Meaningless Propositions*: are a priori true or false
      2.1.1 *Tautologies*: are always true
      2.1.2 *Contradictions*: are always false
   2.2 *Nonsensical Propositions*: are neither true nor false

3.3 Negation in Simple Propositions

Propositions can include negations of various forms, such as: "This watch is not running," "Whales are not fishes," or "This problem is insoluble." Negation and its meaning in a proposition or a group of propositions is one of the chief subjects of formal logic. Here we limit ourselves to our everyday, intuitive knowledge about negation, and only give a brief description of its role when propositions supply pictures.

According to Wittgenstein, negation does not appear at all in the picture that a proposition supplies.

Remember the dual function of a proposition. First, it gives a picture. Second, it asserts the truth of that picture. Negation itself cannot appear in the picture; there is nothing in reality that corresponds to it. It does not even turn the picture into a sort of negative picture, comparable to a photographic negative. Take the proposition "The letter is on the notepad." The corresponding negative picture would be something like "The notepad is on the letter." But the negated proposition says "The letter is not on the notepad." In this proposition, the picture elements, apart from the negation, are the same as those occurring in the original phrase. But the second function of the proposition has been changed by the negation: The assertion of truth is reversed.

Affirmation and negation when applied to the contents of a proposition are called *logical constants* analogously to the mathematical idea of constants. Indeed, when a mathematical variable is multiplied by a nonzero constant, a new variable is obtained that preserves all the essential characteristics of the original variable, such as the position of extreme values. For a proposition, affirmation and negation play a part analogous to that played in mathematics by multiplication of a variable by $+1$ and by -1, respectively. Multiplication by the constant $+1$ leaves the variable unaltered, while the constant -1 leads to a reversal of the sign of values of the variable.

Affirmation and negation are also called *logical operations*, and their symbols are called *logical operators*. In mathematics, an operator is the name for a symbol that, when placed before an expression, specifies that a certain operation is applied to that expression. The use of the names "operation" and "operator" therefore implies that the logician does not consider affirmation or negation as part of the picture furnished by a proposition. On the contrary, it is considered as an instruction to perform a particular mental act upon the picture as a whole.

3.4 Compound Propositions by Logical Operations

In the discussion to follow, we frequently refer to compound propositions and their component propositions. For brevity and clarity, we shorten the term "component propositions" to "components."

Logicians have thoroughly investigated the compound propositions where the truth of one of the components is in some way combined with the truth of another component. An example compound proposition is "If this glass falls to the ground, then it will break." The components "The glass falls to the ground" and "It will break" are said to be included in a single proposition by means of a logical operation.

3.4 Compound Propositions

From simple propositions, we have already become acquainted with the logical operations of affirmation and negation. They assert, respectively, the truth or falsity of the picture conveyed by the proposition.

One can express this also in another way: An affirmative proposition—the affirmation can be either specially mentioned or silently taken for granted—is indeed true if the conveyed picture is a true one. A negative proposition—the negation always needs to be specially mentioned—is indeed true if the conveyed picture is false.

The above discussion may seem unnecessarily complicated, but it makes it easier to understand the subsequent developments.

Only two assertions can be made about the truth of a simple proposition: "It is true" or "It is false." We therefore say that simple propositions have only two *truth possibilities*. Now a group containing two propositions has the following four truth possibilities:

(1) Both propositions are true.
(2) The first proposition is true, the second false.
(3) The first proposition is false, the second true.
(4) Both propositions are false.

So at least four different assertions can be made about the truth of two propositions. Each of these four assertions results from a particular kind of connection between the two simple propositions. As an example, let us consider the following two simple propositions:

(a) The wind is from the east.
(b) The sun is shining.

If the first assertion in the list of truth possibilities is made with respect to these two propositions, then the logical operation called conjunction is employed. Thus, propositions (a) and (b) are linked together by the grammatical conjunction "and." The resulting compound proposition—also called combined or complex—is: "The wind is from the east, and the sun is shining."

This compound proposition, by its use of the word "and," claims to be true if the original propositions (a) and (b) are both true. Hence, the word "and" expresses assertion (1) in our table and rejects assertions (2), (3), and (4). It claims that the compound proposition is false if, in fact, the wind is from the east without the sun shining (2), or the wind is not from the east and the sun is shining (3), or the wind is not from the east and the sun is not shining (4).

The three assertions (2), (3), and (4) are also readily expressed by compound propositions. For example, assertion (4) is handled by "Neither is the wind from the east nor is the sun shining." Indeed, linking the two propositions (a) and (b) by "neither ... nor ..." claims that the compound proposition is true if it is the case that original propositions (a) and (b) are false; and it claims that the compound proposition is false in all three of the other cases.

Notice that each of the four compound propositions contains not one but four assertions—that is, one assertion about the condition under which it is true, and three assertions under which it is false.

The four kinds of compound propositions we have discussed so far are not the only ones that can be formed by the use of assertions (1)–(4). Indeed, instead of declaring a single one of these four assertions to be true and the other three to be false, additional compound propositions choose several of the four at once and assert the truth of the compound proposition if any chosen one is true. We explore these cases while discussing compound propositions formed with "or."

First, we note that "or" is used with two distinct meanings. There is an *inclusive* "or," which means one or the other, or both together; and an *exclusive* "or," which means either one or the other, but not both together.

Suppose our desk lamp fails to work. When we say "The bulb is burned out, or the current has failed," we mean the inclusive "or," since both cases are possible.

The use of the inclusive "or" makes the compound proposition assert that one of assertions (1)–(3) of the table is true, and assertion (4) is false.

On the other hand, when we say "We are going to bed now, or we are going for a walk," we have the exclusive "or" in mind, for we cannot do both at once. This "or" asserts that the compound proposition is true if one of the assertions (2) and (3) in our table is true, and (1) and (4) are false.

The four truth possibilities that occur in a proposition with two components enable us to form a total of 16 groups of conditions in which the compound proposition is true; each of these groups, as we have seen, is composed of four individual conditions called truth conditions. Of course not all these 16 groups occur in everyday speech. The most frequently used of them are as follows:

Conjunction ("and")
Disjunction (inclusive "or")
Alternative (exclusive "or")
Implication ("if ... then ...")
Equivalence ("is the same as")
Incompatibility ("is inconsistent with")

Unfortunately, these designations have not been internationally standardized; for example, one finds disjunction and alternative confused with each other.

For k components, there are $2^k = 2 \cdot 2 \cdot \ldots \cdot 2$ (k times) truth possibilities. For example, $k = 3$ results in $2^3 = 2 \cdot 2 \cdot 2 = 8$ truth possibilities, and $k = 4$ in $2^4 = 16$. The number of truth conditions that can be formed from these truth possibilities increases even more rapidly, and therewith the number of compound propositions which can be formed from the components. From k components, $2^{(2^k)} = 2 \cdot 2 \cdot \ldots \cdot 2$ (2^k times) compound propositions are possible. For $k = 3$, that number is $2^{(2^3)} = 256$, and for $k = 4$ it is $2^{(2^4)} = 65,536$. Of course, only a portion of these have any practical importance.

Here is an example of a compound proposition formed from four components:

(a) *Either* we go on working *and* (b) let our pension rights increase, *or* (c) we retire now *and* (d) lead a healthier life.

Here components (a) and (b) on one hand, and (c) and (d) on the other hand, are each part of a conjunction, and these two conjunctions in turn form part of an alternative. The compound proposition effectively selects six out of the 16 truth possibilities, which means that the compound proposition is to be true if any one of six possibilities is fulfilled, and that it asserts its own falsity for each of the other 10.

A compound proposition says something about two or more facts at once. Its components sketch pictures of each of the facts involved. The grammatical connections then imply an assertion about coexistence or non-coexistence of these facts.

It is impossible to see by inspection if the assertion is true or not; it has to be compared with reality, in the same way as has to be done with a simple proposition and its assertion of being true.

Accordingly, the compound proposition only has meaning if it is verifiable. For this, it is necessary and sufficient that the pictures presented by the components can be compared with reality.

Among compound propositions, there are likewise tautologies and contradictions—that is, propositions that need no comparison with reality, since they are either always true or always false, respectively, regardless of the state of reality. These

3.4 COMPOUND PROPOSITIONS

propositions contain no information; they are only apparently propositions.

There are two causes that make a compound proposition tautologous or contradictory.

First, the compound proposition may be tautologous if it claims truth for all truth possibilities of its components. And it is contradictory if it maintains the falsity of all the truth possibilities of its constituents.

Here is an example using the two simple propositions "Our work is successful" and "We drink coffee." From these we form the tautologous proposition: "That our work is successful if we do not drink coffee does not imply that it is successful if we do drink coffee." This gives no information at all, neither whether we really do drink coffee, nor whether coffee improves our work. Yet the simple components are not themselves tautologous, though the compound of them has this feature, and would still be tautologous if we substituted any other pair of simple phrases. This is so, because the components are joined in a particular manner. The example also shows that meaningless propositions are by no means necessarily useless. They may exemplify logical rules—in particular, ones that we sometimes ignore in our daily life.

Second, the components may be related in certain ways and only certain truth possibilities can occur. Then the compound proposition is a tautology if it claims truth for all such truth possibilities, and is a contradiction if it claims falsity.

As an example, consider the compound proposition that has the form of an implication: "If the purchasing power of money falls, then prices rise." This is a tautology, because its two components, though differently expressed, say the same thing. For another example, the conjunction "These birds are entirely herbivorous, and hence they feed upon insects" is a contradiction, because its two components flatly contradict each other.

In Chapter 2 we asked ourselves whether compound propositions, as contrasted with simple propositions, can communicate something other than facts. This question can now be partially answered for compound propositions that are formed by means of logical operations.

We have seen that these propositions can be arranged in a uniform manner according to the ways in which the truth possibilities of the components are utilized in the truth conditions of the compound proposition.

In mathematics, the logician says that the truth of the compound proposition is a function—the *truth function*—of the truth of the individual components. The components are the arguments—the *truth arguments*—of this function.

If we just know how many components are given, then we know the number of their truth possibilities as well as the number of possible truth conditions. That information gives us the number of compound propositions that can possibly be created from them.

Consider any one of these compound propositions. Regardless of its specific form, the pictures of the components are not somehow worked into a new picture that is not foreseen from those of the components. Instead, the compound proposition only asserts something about the possible simultaneous validity of the individual pictures.

> *We can never reach a form of proposition of which we can say, "Well! That anything like this should be the case was quite impossible to foresee."* (Wittgenstein's diary, November 21, 1916)

It follows that the formation of compound propositions via logical operations cannot ever carry us out of the realm of facts, that is, of relations between the things in the world.

We claim that the same conclusion holds when compound propositions are formed with hitherto unmentioned logical operations of drawing conclusions or giving reasons, indicated by words such as "therefore" and "because."

We omit complete arguments, since they would necessitate discussion of further details of formal logic. But we briefly mention that the formation of compound propositions with the grammatical conjunction "because" is not employed solely to assign purely logical reasons, as in "This number is not divisible by 4 because it is a prime number." Indeed, it is also used to assert a cause-and-effect relation between two facts—for example, "The room is warm because the stove is burning." Derivatively, it is employed to assert a motive-and-action relation in the case of persons—for example, "We are not going to work because we feel ill."

Yet even in these not purely logical ways of giving reasons, it seems impossible that they could lead us out of the domain of the physical or psychological facts expressed in the components.

3.5 Universal Propositions

Propositions are universal when they include generalizing words such as "every," "everywhere," or "always." Even though they may be simple propositions in a grammatical sense, in Wittgenstein's view they involve a logical operation, discussed next.

Such propositions do not depict any facts that can be directly observed in the world. For example, a general fact is expressed in the law of gravitation. It says that every body attracts every other body. That law cannot be directly observed as a fact. Instead, we find that the sun and the earth attract each other, as do the earth and the moon; we also find that bodies on earth attract each other, whether they are made of stone, metal or anything else, and that not only is this now the case, but must have been the case in past ages. We are therefore faced with a series of statements that can be continued indefinitely.

Now the grammatically simple, universal proposition asserts that these statements are all jointly valid; thus, it is a kind of abbreviation of a compound proposition of a particular sort—namely, a conjunction with indefinitely many members.

In a genuine compound proposition, the components furnish pictures of a finite number of facts. Instead of this, a universal proposition gives the listener or reader an instruction that enables construction of the components. In the proposition "All humans are mortal," a person can successively substitute for "all humans" the individuals belonging to the class of humans—in particular, relatives, ancestors, descendants, and so on. The proposition also instructs the person to bind together the resulting components by the word "and."

The general nature of a statement is not always expressed by a special sign of generality, such as "all." Thus, instead of "all humans" we could have simply said "humans."

The signs of generality, whether explicit or not, are in some sense comparable to the mathematical signs for infinite series, which similarly do not supply the user with the individual members of the series, but describe how to construct them.

Since the universal propositions are nothing but abbreviations of conjunctions, they can only communicate facts, and nothing else.

In this context we recall—see Chapter 1—that the facts in the world are not connected by any inner necessity. That conclusion does not rule out the formation of meaningful generalizations. On the contrary, it makes such formation possible, since simple as well as compound propositions have meaning only if they can also be false.

At first sight, it may not be apparent that many compound propositions of everyday language belong to the above types. Often, propositions—even in scientific texts—express not only a piece of factual information, but also—woven into them—the feelings of the speaker or writer. In particular, a proposition may be so formulated that it steers the attention of the listener or reader to what the author considers the more important points. For example, if a logical conjunction of propositions is unexpected or amazing, the author may use the words "but" or "although" instead of "and."

3.6 Propositions About Intentions

In everyday speech, there are other compound propositions that we have not dealt with so far. They ascribe an opinion, a fear, a desire, or an act of will to a person—in brief, what philosophers call an *intention*.

An example is "Monsieur Dupont desires that Pompidou be elected president." Obviously, this is a reasonable proposition, and yet it seems to convey information about something that, in Wittgenstein's view, ought not to exist at all and thus cannot be communicated. Indeed, it appears to communicate not a fact—which is a connection between things—but a connection between a thing and a fact. The thing is Monsieur Dupont. The fact is that Pompidou be elected president.

Bertrand Russell held this view about the time when the Tractatus was written. The clashing claim of the Tractatus that all propositions are pictures of facts, forced Wittgenstein to pay special attention to this kind of proposition.

According to Wittgenstein, Russell's interpretation of intentional propositions is erroneous and based on a suggestive process rooted in everyday speech. We can free ourselves from this influence only by an analysis of these propositions. They deal with complex things—indeed, with complex mental things. We have seen in Chapter 2 that such propositions can be reduced to simpler propositions concerning the components of these complex things. Indeed, we started from propositions about properties and arrived at propositions about pure facts.

Let us consider what exactly can be communicated about the intentions of a person. To begin with, we can speak of a particular activity of the mind, such as wishing or fearing, which cannot be further analyzed. Second, we can mention the mental process of imagining what is wished or feared. Of course, the complex events in those images do not wander about as mere accompaniments of the activities of the mind, but are intimately connected with them. Indeed, there is no wishing or fearing without imagining something wished or feared.

This dry enumeration of the two components of an intention does not purport to establish any psychological or metaphysical hypothesis about mental acts; we only wish to mentally separate the two components. We are entitled to do this, because we can make separate and meaningful statements about each of them. Indeed, mental activities of one kind, such as fearing, can be linked with quite different imagined objects, such as a car accident or being dismissed from one's job. Conversely, different mental activities such as hoping and fearing can be coupled with identical imagined objects. For example, a farmer hoping for rain and a tourist fearing rain may have the same imaginations of wet earth and coolness.

The imagined complex arising from an intention is evidently the picture of a fact—sometimes a true picture, sometimes a false one. That picture can be represented by a speech picture.

The process is analogous to the following. We have a painting of a landscape. We take a photograph of the painting, and thus obtain a secondary representation of the landscape.

In an intentional proposition, the component introduced by the grammatical conjunction "that" is a speech picture of an imagined picture that accompanies the mental act; it is therefore a secondary picture of a fact.

3.6 Propositions About Intentions

But what is the whole compound proposition?

Bertrand Russell interpreted the proposition "Monsieur Dupont desires that Pompidou be elected president" as if the words "desires that" expressed the joining of two propositions in the manner we encountered previously with logical operations. That is, the words "desires that" are treated like "says that" or "is incompatible with." The result is a compound grammatical conjunction.

Suppose we adopt that viewpoint. Then this compound conjunction asserts a relation between "Dupont," the name of an object, and "Pompidou is elected," a proposition that pictures a fact. But then the compound proposition expresses a relation between a thing and a fact, which contradicts the picture theory.

In contrast, Wittgenstein would interpret the compound proposition as follows: In Dupont, an act of will is occurring, *and* the imagined picture involved in this act says the same thing as the speech picture "Pompidou is elected."

Consequently, the intentional proposition is an abbreviation for the logical conjunction of the following two statements:

(1) A certain mental movement is occurring in the stream of consciousness of a person.
(2) The imagined picture belonging to this movement is correctly reproduced by the picture supplied by the component introduced by "that."

The second assertion can also be formulated in the terminology of the picture theory as follows: The picture elements of the imagined picture can be correlated with the elements of the proposition following "that." Thereby, the connections existing in the imagined picture, which are facts, can be correlated with the relations existing in the proposition following "that."

> [T]his does not involve a correlation of a fact with an object, but rather the correlation of facts by means of the correlation of their objects. (Tractatus 5.542)

Communications about intentions are implicit in compound propositions formed by means of the grammatical conjunction "in order that" or any phrase having the same meaning. Take the proposition "We set the alarm clock in order to be awakened at 6 am." This is to be regarded as a conjunction of the following three components:

(1) We set the alarm clock for 6 am.
(2) If we set the alarm clock for 6 am, we will wake up at 6 am.
(3) We wish to wake up at 6 am.

The third of these propositions is to be interpreted in the manner set out above for intentional propositions.

We draw the following conclusion from all we have said about compound propositions: *No compound proposition can be invented that goes beyond the communication possibilities of simple propositions and communicates anything other than facts—that is, relations between the things of the world.*

The next chapter applies the above result to philosophy and shows that many philosophical claims are meaningless.

This is demonstrated using pseudoproblems of philosophy—that is, problems where the formulation is already meaningless.

Chapter 4

Misuse of Language

4.1 Colloquial and Scientific Misuses

This chapter draws conclusions from the results of the picture theory—in particular, from the necessary conditions that a meaningful proposition must obey, and, equally important, from the limits of what a proposition can express.

In daily speech, in professional activities, in fiction, in political speeches, and in sermons we encounter numerous misuses of speech that lead to meaningless or nonsensical assertions. These misuses are sometimes deliberate, whether in jest or from evil intent.

More important for present purposes are abuses of language that occur unnoticed by the speaker or writer. They can even be found in scientific practice.

As a general rule, little harm is done when such meaningless or nonsensical propositions arise from careless formulation of correctly observed circumstances.

The situation is worse if the relations claimed by a proposition are not yet clearly known, and indeed cannot possibly be known. If such propositions do not directly conflict with the grammatical rules of daily speech, then they can hold their ground for a long time and hinder the progress of knowledge.

Indeed, we have seen in Chapter 3 how unverifiable, and therefore meaningless, propositions arise in science; the example concerns assertions of scientists before Einstein's time about the absolute simultaneity of events, through the uncritical use of a concept of simultaneity that at the time was sufficiently precise for use in daily life.

For several decades, the idea of the ether produced similar confusion. But then it was noticed that no statement about it was verifiable, and that any supposition that some substance was acting as support for electromagnetic waves, might as well be abandoned.

Such lapses in thought and speech occur in all sciences. Yet there is a whole discipline which principally supports itself by the misuse of language. This is philosophy.

4.2 Traditional Philosophy

In ancient times, "philosophy" simply meant science. A large portion of Aristotle's writings is devoted to questions of natural science.

However, in the course of history, the sciences have become more and more independent of philosophy. Yet the frontiers separating them remained rather blurred. In 1687, Isaac Newton could still call his book about universal gravity *Philosophiae Naturalis Principia Mathematica*. During the eighteenth century, the philosopher Immanuel Kant took a lively interest in cosmogony, the science dealing with the origin of the universe.

But then areas of science split off from philosophy. For example, during the nineteenth century, psychology divided into two parts. One was called *rational* and continued to form part of philosophy. The other was an empirically based science of psychology. Similarly, logic began to assert its independence. Mathematicians like Augustus De Morgan and George Boole furnished decisive impulses to its further development.

At the time Wittgenstein wrote the Tractatus, philosophy, generally speaking, claimed to deal with the following spheres.

The *Theory of Knowledge* tries to answer the question how our knowledge, both in daily life and in scientific matters, comes into existence and when it can be considered to be valid. Hence, it investigates the phenomenon of consciousness by examining the connection between consciousness and its objects, while ignoring the psychological and physiological conditions of consciousness.

Metaphysics deals with objects of which we neither have nor can have any empirical knowledge, but which since ancient times humans have thought important to comprehend. It attempts to grasp by intellectual processes what is important about existence, the soul, and God.

Ethics and *Aesthetics* have as their object the realm of values. What has value, and why? What is morally good? What is aesthetically beautiful?

The *Philosophy of Life* purports to direct a person's attention to her own being and her position in the cosmos; it inquires into the meaning of life—indeed, of existence in general.

The *Philosophical Basis of the Sciences* examines the epistemological—that is, knowledge-theoretical—underpinnings of individual sciences. In particular, it investigates the manner in which sciences develop terms, criteria, and proofs.

Logic, when taught in faculties of philosophy of universities, investigates the criteria applicable to correct thinking, irrespective of the special content of thought.

However, to an increasing degree, logic was dealt with in faculties of mathematics, in the form of symbolic or modern logic based on the work of Gottlob Frege, Giuseppe Peano, David Hilbert, Kurt Gödel, and many others. Similarly, the philosophical basis of science in the theory of knowledge was handled by the individual sciences. In the last third of the nineteenth century, the names Heinrich Hertz, Wilhelm Wundt, Henri Poincaré, and Ernst Mach deserve special mention.

Philosophy, in the sense in which it is today most widely understood, and indeed itself claims to be understood, is the endeavor to find a solution to the problems listed above by means of rational thought. This excludes any recourse to sentimental arguments, intuition, religious revelation, or common sense. Its aim is not reached until its results have been expressed in propositions.

Here are two pairs of mutually contradictory philosophical propositions. For brevity and clarity, we have reduced parts of the original statements.

The first pair is taken from Rudolf Carnap's *Scheinprobleme in der Philosophie* (Pseudoproblems of Philosophy).

(1) The *realist* thesis: "The corporeal things that we perceive around us are not only the content of our perceptions but also exist by themselves."

(2) The *idealist* thesis: "What is real is not the outside world itself; only the perceptions and imaginings that we have about it are real."

The second pair comes from ethics and concerns the thesis of utilitarianism and the formal ethics of Immanuel Kant.

(3) The *utilitarian* thesis: "The highest aim of moral behavior is the greatest happiness of the greatest number of mankind."

(4) Kant's *formal ethics*: "Act so that the maxim accepted by your will could always be valid as the principle of a general legislation."

4.3 Inadmissibility of Philosophical Propositions

According to Wittgenstein's conclusions about the limits of what can be expressed in language, we must contest the right of philosophy to set up propositions of the kind just given, for none of the claimed themes concern facts.

Of course, books of philosophy are not always devoid of concrete descriptions of situations. For instance, varieties of moral behavior may be elucidated. Or events and experiences may be recounted that give rise to particular feelings and attitudes toward the world and life. For example, Jean-Paul Sartre explained his ideas in a whole series of novels. Yet the object of the decisive theses of philosophy is not facts, and it is not relations between the things in the world. Therefore, the resulting propositions cannot really have any meaning nor contain any information, even though they may appear to say something.

Even before Wittgenstein there was fundamental criticism of philosophy. Indeed, even philosophers declared whole sections of philosophy to be pseudosciences. The most radical among them in recent centuries was David Hume, with his rejection of all science not built up upon sense experience; and perhaps the most profound was Immanuel Kant, who rejected all metaphysical speculation about God, the soul, and the world.

Wittgenstein's criticism goes even further. It embraces the whole of philosophy; a philosophical statement without exception is either meaningless or nonsensical. This is so whether we can identify faults of reasoning or not. The very questions philosophy asks are absurd.

> *Most of the propositions and questions to be found in philosophical works are not false but nonsensical. Consequently, we cannot give any answer to questions of this kind, but can only establish that they are nonsensical. Most of the propositions and questions of philosophers arise from our failure to understand the logic of our language.* (Tractatus 4.003)

Faced with the attempts of traditional philosophy to make statements about values, consciousness, the meaning of the world, and so on, we find ourselves in a situation comparable to that of a technician or examiner in a patent office to whom today, long after the discovery of the principle of conservation of energy, an invention is offered that claims to produce perpetual motion. The examiner is entitled to reject any such patent application, without any obligation to refer in detail to the defective logic. And this despite the fact that the description of the invention may be precisely worked out, and that the inventor likely will charge the examiner with intellectual arrogance.

The comparison is imperfect, since the statements in patent applications may have perfectly precise meaning, which makes it possible to prove their falsity. In contrast, philosophical theses contain no genuine, informative statements capable of being true or false, even though they may appear to be meaningful.

Let us consider the two pairs of theses (1)–(4) quoted above from this viewpoint. It must be stressed that our sole purpose here is to explain Wittgenstein's critique, and that our all too simple exposition doesn't do justice to the philosophers' earnest striving after knowledge.

In the spirit of Wittgenstein, Rudolf Carnap analyzed theses (1) and (2) quoted earlier with exemplary clarity and penetration.

In these theses, the words "exist" and "real" occur. In everyday life, when we say that an object does or doesn't exist, we mean the object can or can't be observed at a certain place and time.

This empirical meaning of "exist" is demonstrated in the following three propositions:

(a) "The positron—the positively charged counterpart of an electron—exists." Indeed, experiments by Carl D. Anderson proved Paul Dirac's conjecture.
(b) "The castle of Berlin did not exist in 1960." It was destroyed during World War II, reconstructed 2013–2019.
(c) "Centaurs do not exist."

The empirical idea of existence or reality can be applied to all things in the world, whether physical or mental; in the case of the latter, at least the time and circumstances of their occurrence can be stated. Statements including these ideas are factual statements, for they assert the existence of temporal and spatial connections of one thing with other things.

But this kind of existence is certainly not meant in the two philosophical theses concerning the outside world. The theses deny or assert that the world outside us is a hallucination. A mentally ill person might face the same predicament when deciding whether a certain perception is a hallucination. But in principle that person could establish by himself whether the perception is faulty by comparing it with his other perceptions. Among such perceptions, there might be words he hears from trustworthy friends. But the kind of reality which is affirmed or denied by theses (1) and (2) cannot be tested that way.

There is also a metaphorical meaning of the word "exist" in which it is applied even to mental objects, as in the proposition "There exist pairs of whole numbers for which the sum of their squares is itself the square of a whole number." Or in the statement "There exists no solution to this problem." Here, the phrase "something exists" means that something can be constructed or proved by logical considerations. But this, too, is not meant in the two theses quoted above.

In the absence of any direct definition of a word, it is also possible to fix its meaning by stating a criterion of truth for the propositions in which the word is employed; that is, it must be clearly stated which facts, if verified, involve the truth of such a proposition, and which other facts, if verified, involve its falsity. That way, psychotherapy can speak in a meaningful way of mental processes or conditions that at present cannot be observed. For example, one may talk about an anxiety complex. This notion does not require us to torture our minds in trying to imagine something in the brain; we only need to clearly establish the settings in which anxiety surfaces in a patient.

This minimum requirement is not satisfied when the word "exist" or "real" is used in the two philosophical theses. No one can say what our experiences or perceptions have to be if either of the two theses is true. The theses are therefore pseudostatements. If anything at all is expressed by them, it cannot be an informative communication but at most a feeling in the mind, an attitude, or a way of imagining the outer world. The theses try to communicate something which is not communicable, something which perhaps could find adequate expression in a lyric poem.

The ethical theses (3) and (4) quoted above are a different case. They have a clear meaning, insofar as they express a wish. Such a wish is undoubtedly implied; no ethical philosopher would deny the desire to see the content of a thesis realized. The theses might also express the will of a legislator or the will of God. But that is not what they are intended to do. They are primarily meant to be statements—in fact, statements about an absolute moral obligation. An ethical thesis is an attempt to state what a person ought to do, and the considerations by a writer on ethics are intended to give reasons why a person is morally bound to do it.

At least in the fully worked out systems of traditional ethics, this does not mean the psychological or sociological causes for the voice of conscience and our tendency to follow it; indeed, it means something that is outside all causes and effects.

If propositions about moral obligation, goodness, or moral values are genuine statements, it must be possible to state what is the case if they are true, and what is the case if they are false. This demand about the truth criterion of the thesis must not be confused with the question of what happens if the thesis is obeyed and what happens if it is not obeyed. An ethical thesis claims to be valid even if no one obeys it. But there is no way of knowing where to look for a criterion of the truth or falsity of such a thesis.

Therefore, if an ethical thesis tries to express anything more than a mere *opinion* about value, then it is a pseudostatement. This is always true of propositions dealing with values. Facts, the only possible objects of communication, contain no value, and among propositions dealing with facts there is no hierarchy. For they all necessarily stem from elementary propositions, which are all of equal value.

If there are any values—and Wittgenstein doesn't deny this at all—they are not in the world of facts; that is, they do not exist in the world at all.

> *The sense of the world must lie outside the world. In the world, everything is as it is, and everything happens as it does happen; in it no value exists—and if it did exist, it would have no value.*
> *If there is any value that does have value, it must lie outside the whole sphere of what happens and is the case. For all that happens and is the case is accidental.* (Tractatus 6.41)

> *Therefore, there cannot be propositions of ethics. Propositions can express nothing that is higher.* (Tractatus 6.42)

We can indeed follow a system of ethics in our lives; we can also attract others to it by our example, or by helping them to bring out neglected feelings and suppressed urges. We can also describe what kinds of behavior are prejudicial to the security of human society, but we cannot by logical means give reasons for a moral obligation.

> *It is clear that ethics cannot be put into words.* (Tractatus 6.421)

4.4 Inadmissible Questions

Humans expect from verbal propositions, especially from scientific ones, something that propositions cannot do. People want to say, or to be told, why and for what purpose they are in the world, what they ought to do, and what happens to them when they die.

Meaningful answers can only be expected to meaningful questions, and questions are only meaningful when they are about the existence or nonexistence of facts in the world. But the things that trouble us simply cannot be expressed in the form of such questions.

Little by little, science answers all genuine questions dealing with things, but then leaves us alone. Beyond that point, philosophy—mistakenly used as a source of information—can only give us pseudoanswers. Genuine philosophical reflection, free of illusion, guides us to see that there are no remaining questions to be answered, but tasks for us to do.

> *We feel that even when all possible scientific questions have been answered, the problems of living remain completely untouched. Of course, there are then no questions left, and this itself is the answer.* (Tractatus 6.52)

> *The solution of the riddle of life in space and time lies outside space and time.*
> *(Indeed, problems that are not part of natural science must be solved.)* (Tractatus 6.4312)

Every person must seek the solution in actively coming to terms with life. Knowledge of the facts in the world will not help to find the solution.

> *All the facts are solely part of the problem, and not part of its solution.* (Tractatus 6.4321)

The solution is life itself.

> *The solution of the problem of life is seen in the vanishing of the problem.*
> *(Isn't this the reason why persons to whom the meaning of life became clear after a long struggle with doubts, could not tell what that meaning consisted of?)* (Tractatus 6.521)

The world of possible communications is limited by what we can think. This limit has only one side, the one turned toward

4.4 Inadmissible Questions

us. A wish to formulate the question of what lies beyond this limit already contains the impossible attempt to cross it.

This is not to say that there does not exist anything uncommunicable, anything that cannot be put into words. We have already found such things: They are the elementary things. For us, they are certain a priori; they make themselves manifest. But neither their nature nor their very existence can be expressed in propositions.

Logical necessities also manifest themselves, but in another way. They do so in propositions formed with logical correctness; but they themselves cannot be explained or proved in propositions.

> *Proof in logic is merely a mechanical expedient for easier recognition of tautologies in complicated cases.* (Tractatus 6.1262)

In an even stronger sense, it is impossible to put into words experiences concerning the existence of the world and our own conscious life, its meaning or meaninglessness—in any but a logical sense—or about our moral destiny.

> *There are, indeed, things that cannot be put into words. They* make themselves manifest. *They are what is mystical.* (Tractatus 6.522)

Such things can be more important to us than anything that can be put into words. So it is for Wittgenstein, and he showed it in his life. He only mentions it in the Tractatus in order to urge us to be consistent and not relate—in an inadmissible and useless manner—the mystical to the world of facts, which is all that can be expressed in words:

> *It is not* how *things are in the world that is mystical, but that it exists.* (Tractatus 6.44)

> *How things are in the world is a matter of complete indifference for what is higher. God does not reveal himself in the world.* (Tractatus 6.432)

We get no nearer to what is higher by trying to put anything about it into words. This only results in nonsense.

> *What we cannot speak about, we must pass over in silence.*
> (Tractatus 7)

Philosophy cannot give us things of existence, so to speak. Even deep and obscure formulations cannot capture anything where all is feeling and guessing:

> *Everything that can be thought at all can be thought clearly. Everything that can be put into words can be put clearly.*
> (Tractatus 4.116)

So what role is then left for philosophy to play? The next chapter gives Wittgenstein's answer: Philosophy is to help achieve clarity when language is misused in meaningless questions and claims.

Chapter 5

Genuine Philosophy

5.1 Tasks of Philosophy

What field of activity is left for philosophy after all that has been said? The search for facts must be left to the individual sciences. Investigation of a priori truths concerns logic and mathematics. Philosophy cannot even establish propositions.

> *Philosophy aims at the logical clarification of thoughts.*
> *Philosophy is not a body of doctrine but an activity.*
> *A philosophical work consists essentially of elucidations.*
> *Philosophy does not result in "philosophical propositions," but rather in the clarification of propositions.*
> *Without philosophy, thoughts are, as it were, cloudy and indistinct; its task is to make them clear and to give them sharp boundaries.* (Tractatus 4.112)

The propositions to be clarified by philosophy are above all those of the sciences. Philosophy investigates the formation of concepts and thoughts that the sciences make use of, the usefulness of hypotheses, and the criteria for judging the truthfulness of statements and theories.

In this sense, the theory of knowledge is the philosophy of psychology; it should inquire what is the meaning of concepts such as "I," "the outer world," and "the will"; and to decide whether relations put forward about these concepts have any meaning.

Wittgenstein's fundamental considerations about the meaning of propositions, about truth and falsity—which we have only been able to touch on—and his account of the logical notation of concepts are contributions to the philosophy of logic.

Philosophy can make no statement whatever about the general problems of existence that traditionally sustained metaphysics. But philosophy can render a valuable service to inquirers by deciding which questions have meaning and can therefore be answered, and which are nonsensical.

A spiritual liberation ensues when problems such as those concerning death—presented in the guise of questions—are relegated to their place among practical tasks.

In the past, questions about what lies beyond the world were mixed together with questions about facts. The contribution of philosophy consists of separating these two types of questions.

5.2 Philosophy and the Tractatus

Philosophy now faces an almost insoluble problem. When we decide and reason why something can or cannot be put into words, doesn't that imply that we are attempting to say something that cannot be said?

If philosophy is to act consistently, only an indirect approach remains open:

> *It must set limits to what cannot be thought, by working outwards through what can be thought.* (Tractatus 4.114)

> *It will signify what cannot be said, by presenting clearly what can be said.* (Tractatus 4.115)

Consistently implemented, we arrive at a quite unusual method for philosophizing:

> *The correct method in philosophy would really be the following: to say nothing except what can be said—that is, propositions of natural science, which have nothing to do with philosophy; and then, whenever another person wanted to say something metaphysical, to prove to him that he had failed to give a meaning to certain signs in his propositions.*

5.2 Philosophy and the Tractatus

*Although it would not be satisfying to the other person—he would not have the feeling that we were teaching him philosophy—*this *method would be the only strictly correct one.* (Tractatus 6.53)

In the first line of the quotation, Wittgenstein says "would really be," for he himself in the Tractatus does not adhere to this method. If we exclude the parts of the Tractatus dealing with logical connections in the narrower sense—about one third of the book—we encounter philosophical propositions at every step.

For instance, consider the assertion that everything we encounter can be analyzed into facts and things; that assertion is of decisive importance for the entire work.

The matter under discussion is facts, but the possibility of analyzing them into elementary facts and elementary things is not itself a fact. The assertion that this analysis can be effected is not verifiable. This is immediately seen when we attempt to answer the question "What must the appearance of the world be if the assertion is true, and what if it is false?"

On the other hand, the assertion contains no statement which is a priori true. Therefore, according to Wittgenstein's own definition, it is nonsensical.

When we dealt with the picture theory, we already pointed out that it is not demonstrable, but that Wittgenstein gives it as a guide for seeing things correctly. That argument may be acceptable, despite the danger of optical illusion. But the picture theory is to furnish a criterion of whether or not a proposition has meaning.

Yet for use in any concrete case, we should have to know, for example, whether the symbols of a proposition are in their logical form compatible with one another. But with regard to that problem, there is no knowledge in the genuine meaning of that word, namely, factual knowledge.

That concepts such as "triangular" and "painful" cannot be connected to each other is something we *feel*. Even in such a simple case, we can paraphrase in a most general way why the two concepts belong to different categories.

It seems that all this does not meet Wittgenstein's requirement that a philosophical work should consist essentially of elucidations. Here, the meaning of elucidation is somewhat narrower than the usual one: Ideas that cannot be defined or only defined with difficulty—such as the idea of "imagination"—or grammatical forms such as genitive or dative, can be elucidated by forming propositions in which the ideas or forms occur.

A proposition can be elucidated by examples of states of things in which it is true.

An inadmissible conclusion can be elucidated by simply using it once in a significant example; the hearer will see the point without further elaboration.

The propositions used for the purpose of elucidation do not give the explanation but allow it to become visible. Thereupon, we should forget these propositions and only retain what has shown itself in them.

The doubts we have accumulated while reading the Tractatus are treated by Wittgenstein at the end of the book in an altogether surprising manner. He does not remove these doubts; he strengthens them. The reader is told to consider the whole system of propositions of the Tractatus as being only an elucidation—indeed, an elucidation of a very peculiar kind.

These propositions, he says, have in reality no meaning that can be stated. But precisely in the recognition of their meaninglessness, something should dawn upon the reader.

Wittgenstein's intention in the Tractatus is to have an overall settlement of accounts with traditional philosophy, and to show that philosophical propositions are nonsensical. But this is just

5.2 Philosophy and the Tractatus

the sort of thing that cannot be expressed in propositions; it can only be elucidated.

Now the elucidation furnished by the Tractatus consists precisely of the following: The propositions put forth in the course of the investigation of the problem—however enlightening they may appear at first sight—reveal themselves to be nonsensical as a consequence of the investigation itself.

> *My propositions are elucidations in this way: Anyone who understands me eventually recognizes them as nonsensical, when he has used them—as steps—to climb up beyond them. (He must, so to speak, throw away the ladder after he has climbed up on it.)*
> *He must transcend these propositions, and then he will see the world the right way.* (Tractatus 6.54)

This can be paraphrased as follows: Forget these propositions as quickly as possible, and then try again to go back to making philosophical statements—if you can. It can no longer be done.

Appendix A

Time Relations in Physics

Two kinds of facts concern the speed of light that at first sight seem contradictory.

(1) An observer stationed either at the source of light or at a fixed distance from it finds that light spreads out in all directions with equal speed. It doesn'tmatter whether the observer and source of light are in fixed position or have a *common* movement, for example, relative to the earth or relative to the system of fixed stars.

(2) From observation (1) it would follow by common sense that an observer moving toward the source of light must record a greater speed for the light reaching him, and an observer moving away from the source of light must record a lesser speed.

Surprisingly, the light reaching the observer of case (2) always has the same speed. For example, the sun's light reaches us in the morning, when we are moving toward it, at the same speed as in the evening, when we are moving away from it.

The observer who is in motion relative to the source of light will therefore have to consider as false the assertion made by the observer who is at rest relative to the source of light.

Obviously, this contradiction cannot reside in the natural phenomenon itself. It must arise from our applying inadequate concepts to the phenomenon—that is, inadequate concepts of time and distance, since they are used to define speed. These concepts must be further refined if the statements of the two observers are to be compatible with each other.

The refinement is effected by Einstein's special theory of relativity. It supplies formulas for determining distance and time

Appendix A

when relative speeds of the observers are involved. The formulas tell each observer rules to be applied to measurements of length and time when the experience of the other observer is to be computed.

A remarkable result occurs in the case of two events—for example, flashes of light—occurring in two places at a great distance from each other. Suppose we have to decide which event happens first. The decision can be different according to whether the observer is at rest relative to the places where the events occur, or is in motion relative to one of the places or to both of them.

Indeed, according to the observer's state of motion or rest, the two events can be simultaneous, or one or the other can occur first. We have used the word "can" and not "seem(s) to" because there is no criterion for deciding which time relation "actually" exists between the events.

The only way to resolve the supposed discrepancy between the claims of the two observers, is application of the formulas of the special theory of relativity. These formulas say that both observers are right.

The supposition that a real, absolute time relation exists independently of the conditions of the observer is therefore shown to be nonsensical.

Of course, not all events can reverse their succession in time according to the conditions of observation; for this to happen, the events must be close to each other in time, and far apart in space.

The same conclusion applies to any two *causally* connected events; the special theory of relativity says that the one causing the other is the earlier one for *all* observers.

Appendix B

Elementary Things and Facts

Throughout this book, we have used the expressions "elementary things" and "elementary facts," which seem more precise than the words employed by Wittgenstein in the Tractatus. He calls things that cannot be further analyzed simply "things" or "objects," and he calls "complexes" the things we encounter immediately in the world. Relations existing between things he calls "facts," irrespective of whether they consist of simple or composite things.

References

Amery, J., *On Aging*, Indiana University Press, 1994. Originally published as *Über das Altern*, Ernst Klett Verlag, 1968.

Anscombe, G. E. M., *An Introduction to Wittgenstein's Tractatus*, Hutchinson University Library, 1959.

Barnett, L., *The World We Live In*, published by LIFE magazine in 13 installments, 1952-1954.

Carnap, R., *Scheinprobleme in der Philosophie* (Pseudoproblems of Philosophy), 1928, available from Meiner Verlag für Philosophie, 2005.

Fann, K. T., *Wittgenstein's Conception of Philosophy*, Partridge Publishing, 2015.

Friedlander, E., *Signs of Sense*, Harvard University Press, 2001.

Hartnack, J., *Wittgenstein und die moderne Philosophie* (Wittgenstein and Modern Philosophy), Kohlhammer-Verlag, 1962. English edition, Doubleday, 1965.

Lakatos, I., *Proofs and Refutations*, Cambridge University Press, 1976.

Mounce, H. O., *Wittgenstein's Tractatus*, University of Chicago Press, 1981.

Nordmann, A., *Wittgenstein's Tractatus*, Cambridge University Press, 2005.

Stegmüller, W., *Die Hauptströmungen der Gegenwartsphilosophie* (Mainstream Contemporary Philosophy), Humboldt-Verlag, 1952. Revised edition, Kröner, 1960 (title translation by eds.).

White, R. M., *Wittgenstein's 'Tractatus Logico-Philosophicus'*, Continuum International Publishing Group, 2006.

Wittgenstein, L., *Tractatus Logico-Philosophicus*, Routledge and Kegan Paul, Ltd, 1961. Translation by D. F. Pears and B. F. McGuinness, and with the introduction by Bertrand Russell, F.R.S.

About Author and Translator

About the Author

Friedrich Philipp Hülster was born 1905 into a wealthy merchant family in the town of Siegburg, Germany. After high school, he started studying theology at the Catholic-Theological Faculty of the University of Bonn, but then stopped abruptly.

Later he explained, "I just couldn't accept what I was told." He turned to physics, finished with a PhD at the University of Cologne in 1933, and obtained a position at the research lab of the Telefunken Company in Berlin. There he specialized in vacuum tube technology.

In 1938, he married Eva Julie Faßnacht, born in 1906. To their great regret, the couple never had children. Instead, they focused on their nieces and nephews, giving significant material support whenever they saw a need.

In 1933, the conservative, mostly Catholic, Zentrum Party made a Faustian bargain with the Nazis. In return for Zentrum support for the Ermächtigungsgesetz—this law gave Hitler dictatorial power—the Nazis promised that the Catholic Church would remain untouched by the upheaval to come. That law paved the way for the unspeakable crimes of World War II and the Holocaust.

Hülster rejected the Nazi regime. Seeing the savagery of the Kristallnacht in 1938, he came home crying. There was nothing he could do; anybody speaking up after 1933 was arrested and thrown into a concentration camp.

During World War II, he continued to work at the Telefunken lab in Berlin. Miraculously, he and his wife survived the bombing of Berlin and the Soviet Union's conquest and occupation.

In 1947, Hülster fled from Berlin literally overnight to avoid imminent deportation to the Soviet Union. Subsequently, he and his wife moved to France, and he joined the French company Thomson in Paris.

He continued to work on vacuum tube technology, producing—among many other things—a superb amplifier for large-power radio transmitters. By careful selection of alloys and materials he avoided temperature-induced stresses between the individual parts and so achieved an extraordinarily long service life for that amplifier.

By the end of the 1950s, vacuum tubes were on the way out. He was unable to make the transition to the new transistor technology and moved to the patent department of the company. But after a career dedicated to research, he increasingly considered the paper work on patents a drudgery he longed to escape.

This he did at age 63. When queried later how he could retire so early, he said, smilingly, "I played the retirement game correctly"—meaning that time was of the essence, and not money.

When asked what he intended to do after the departure from Thomson, he answered, "I want to understand what can be said."

He began this project by studying the book *Tractatus Logico-Philosophicus* by the philosopher Ludwig Wittgenstein (1889-1951). By now, several books have been written about the Tractatus. Hülster wrote an introduction whose English translation you hold in your hands. As he explains in the preface, writing about the Tractatus was his way of confirming that he had understood the book.

He died 1992 in Bad Neuenahr-Ahrweiler, Germany. His wife Eva passed away four years later, in 1996, also in Bad Neuenahr-Ahrweiler.

About the Translator

W. E. O'Hea was a friend of Hülster's. The editors of this book have been unable to find out details about O'Hea, not even the names behind the initials W and E. But we know that O'Hea lived in Vaucresson near Paris, France, was married, and had at least one child, a girl. He was fluent in German.

It is unknown how he came to translate Hülster's book about the Tractatus, a formidable task. A reasonable guess is that he read the typed copy of the German book, was impressed, and proposed that an English version be created to assure wider distribution.

Subject Index

Amery, Jean, 10
Anderson, C. D., 82
Anscombe, G. E. M., 6
atomism, 16
  logical, 17

Boole, George, 78

Carnap, Rudolf, 80, 82
color wheel, 37
communication
  means, 31
  method
    sense-of-sight, 31
    sign language, 31
    single sign, 32
    speech, 31
    writing, 31
complex, Tractatus definition, 96
cosmogony, 78
curve, simple closed, 38

differentia specifica, 14
Dirac, Paul, 82

Einstein, Albert, 60, 77, 94
elucidation of ideas, 92
ethics, 79
  formal, 80

fact, 12, 13, 38
  chain, 15

elementary, 16
    existence, 16
  non-fact, 17
  Tractatus definition, 96
  unconnectedness, 25
Fann, K. T., 4
form of representation, 40
free will, 27
Frege, Gottlob, 53, 79
Friedlander, Eli, 6

genus proximum, 14
Gödel, Kurt, 79

Hartnack, Justus, 6
Hertz, Heinrich, 79
Hilbert, David, 79
Hume, David, 81

Kant, Immanuel, 78, 80, 81

Lakatos, Imre, 61
language
  misuse
    colloquial, 77
    science, 77
logic
  mathematics, 79
  philosophy, 79
logical
  affirmation, 64
  alternative, 67
  atomism, 16
  constant, 64
  contradiction, 61
  disjunction, 67

equivalence, 67
   form, 24, 40
      picture and reality, 39
   implication, 67
   incompatibility, 67
   necessity, 26
   negation, 63
   operation, 64
   operator, 64
   tautology, 61, 69

Mach, Ernst, 79
McGuinness, B. F., 3
misuse of language, 77
Morgan, Augustus De, 78
Mounce, Howard O., 6
multiplicity, mathematical, 36

name, reference to elements, 57
natural laws, 26
Newton, Isaac, 78
non-fact, 17
Nordmann, Alfred, 6

object
   ideal, 15
   Tractatus definition, 29, 96
observer
   in motion, 94
   stationary, 94

patent claim, analogy for complex proposition, 46
Peano, Giuseppe, 79
Pears, D. F., 3
philosophy
   aesthetics, 79

basis of the sciences, 79
  correct method, 90
  ethics, 79
    formal, 80
  inadmissibility of propositions, 80
  logic, 79
  metaphysics, 79
  of life, 79
  tasks, 89
  theory of knowledge, 78
  traditional, 78
  utilitarianism, 80
picture
  characterization, 35
  link with representation of object, 33
  purely logical, 41
  theory, 33
Poincaré, Henri, 79
principle of verifiability, 59
property, 19
  complex things, 19
  external, 24
  formal, 24
  internal, 24
  two different meanings, 20
proposition
  compound, 64
  contradictory philosophical, 80
  elementary, 45, 46
  formed by logical operations, 64
  intention, 73
  meaningful, 62
  meaningless, 61, 62
  negation, 63
  nonsensical, 62

ordinary, analysis, 46
sense, 57
senseless, 61
sign, 57
   link with fact, 57
simple, 56
structure, 44
universal, 71, 72
pseudo
  -answer, 86
  -proposition, 62
  -statement, 84

question, inadmissible, 85

relation, as thing, 17
Russell, Bertrand, 53, 73

Sartre, Jean-Paul, 81
saying versus showing, 58
showing versus saying, 58
sign(s)
   of generality, 72
   relationship with symbol, 54
special theory of relativity, 94
speed of light, 94
   observer, 94
     in motion, 94
     stationary, 94
Stegmüller, Wolfgang, 17
structure, picture and reality, 36
symbol, link with components of a proposition, 54
syntax, 55
   language, 55
   link with rules defining combinations of words, 55

tautology, 61
thing, 12
  complex, 15
  elementary, 16
    existence, 16
  relations, 13
  substance of the world, 28
  Tractatus definition, 29, 96
  two groups, 12
thought
  link with logical picture of facts, 41
  process, 42
  sense of proposition, 57
time relations in physics, 94
truth possibilities, 65

verifiability, principle, 59
Vienna Circle, 59

White, Roger M., 6
world, 10
Wundt, Wilhelm, 79

Printed in Great Britain
by Amazon